Non-native and Nonstandard Dialect Students

NCTE Committee on Classroom Practices in Teaching English

Candy Carter, *Chair*, Sierra Mountain Intermediate School, Truckee, California
Yetive Bradley, Oakland City Schools, Oakland, California
James C. Lalley, Loyola Academy, Wilmette, Illinois
Patricia Phelan, University City High School, San Diego, California
Jean Procope-Martin, King Philip Middle School, West Hartford, Connecticut

Non-native and Nonstandard Dialect Students

Classroom Practices in Teaching English,
1982–1983

Candy Carter, Chair
and the Committee on Classroom Practices

National Council of Teachers of English
1111 Kenyon Road, Urbana, Illinois 61801

Library of Congress Cataloging in Publication Data

Main entry under title:

Non-native and nonstandard dialect students.

(Classroom practices in teaching English;
1982–1983)
    Includes bibliographical references.
    1. English language—Study and teaching—Foreign students—Addresses, essays, lectures. 2. English language—Study and teaching—Addresses, essays, lectures. 3. English language—Standardization— Addresses, essays, lectures. I. Carter, Candy, 1947- II. National Council of Teachers of English. Committee on Classroom Practices. III. Series.
PE1128.A2N6   1982   428.2'4'071073   82-14502
ISBN 0-8141-3351-7

Contents

Preface

When the Committee on Classroom Practices had its annual meeting in Boston in 1981, we had difficulty at first in identifying a theme that would provide possible solutions to a problem being experienced by all teachers of English/language arts. In the middle of a fairly ho-hum discussion, Ray Rodrigues arrived with an idea, one so obvious we should have thought of it before: the problems faced by the non-native speaker of English or the speaker of nonstandard dialect in the regular English classroom.

Each of us had had the experience of having a new arrival to this country in our class. Yet, we assumed it was a local problem, peculiar to urban areas, or the West Coast, or the East Coast, or the Midwest. Apparently not. America is experiencing a new wave of immigration, and the schools are one of the first places this new wave is evident.

In a sense, the large urban centers are fortunate. They have the numbers of students to justify the creation of English as a Second Language (ESL) classes. In fact, in my first eight years of teaching, when I taught in a 75 percent Hispanic school in which Spanish was the dominant language of approximately one-third of the student body, I rarely encountered a student in my class who was not equipped with a better-than-rudimentary ability in English. It was when I changed teaching positions to a rural mountain community that I began to encounter a more typical situation: A student from Mexico would enroll and be placed in my class. Relying on the help of a few Spanish-speaking students, I would muddle through, with the student probably no more capable in English when the course ended than when it began. Our discussion in Boston led me to the conclusion that my experience was typical, not unique.

After the meeting, the call for manuscripts was issued in *Language Arts, English Journal, Council-Grams, College English,* and *English Education,* as well as in the journals of many NCTE-affiliated organizations.

By 1 April 1982 we had received manuscripts submitted from throughout the United States. The manuscripts, with authors' names removed, were evaluated by committee members Jean Procope-Martin, James Lalley, Patricia Phelan, and Yetive Bradley —a committee representing several geographic areas and grade level viewpoints.

Twenty-four manuscripts representing these varying viewpoints were finally selected and submitted to the NCTE Editorial Board for approval to publish. All of them represent methods of working with the student who is speaking English as a new language or speaking a nonstandard dialect.

Introduction

We have all heard or read the analogy between America and salad bowls and melting pots. The most recent, and in my opinion the most accurate, appraisal of America's make-up is that of a mosaic: Each culture has contributed its own unique tiles, with their distinctive glaze and sharp edges, to the mosaic. Examined too closely, a mosaic presents a discordant picture of poorly, even oddly, juxtaposed individual units strangely cemented together. Yet, on balance, this technique, when viewed from a reasonable distance, presents a complete picture, the total amounting to far more than the sum of the parts.

Acceptance of the tile into the mosaic does not need to entail the loss of its identity, in the same way that entrance into American society of a new group does not necessarily involve a shedding of the old culture. The American mosaic, as it accepts new tiles or groups, simply becomes a larger, more complex, and thus more interesting picture.

What is the cement that bonds this mosaic together? It could be belief in certain ideas, certain ethics. But of what use are these beliefs without the power to express them? The cement in the American mosaic is language, and the cement does not interfere with the distinctiveness of the tile's beauty; rather, it permits each tile to become a part of the whole. Likewise, the non-native or the speaker of nonstandard dialect can be bonded to the American mosaic by developing fluency and competence in standard American English.

All of us of non-English ancestry have forebears who arrived in this country with little or no knowledge of that complex and almost incomprehensible language known as American English. Both of my grandfathers, for example, began school speaking only their parents' native tongue. I remember asking them how they got by, how they survived. Their answer was a distant look, a shrug of the shoulders. They managed; somehow they learned English, and their original language was preserved mainly in songs, Christmas customs, and family expressions.

All of America's new arrivals have had to grapple with survival in an alien land with odd customs and a complex language—and a local citizenry that grizzles about people who "can't speak English." Some of the immigrants found their way alone. Many became part of a colony, be it a Yiddish-speaking ghetto in the Northeast, a Scandinavian farming community in the Midwest, an Asian "town" in the Far West. Others came unwillingly, in chains, forced to abandon their language for that of the slaveholder or boss. Through oppression and isolation, dialects developed, such as "Black English," "pidgin," or "Spanglish."

Between the two World Wars and the Vietnam War, we saw few immigrants. Now the numbers of newcomers are again on the rise, this time principally from the Third World. Yet the problem has not changed. The children of these new arrivals must still undergo that initial American experience: learning the language of the land. We are also left with the legacy of our forefathers' bigotry: We continue to find students whose lack of competence in standard English hampers their ability to become bonded to the American mosaic.

And what of the teacher in this dilemma? Those of us in urban areas may have a class or even an entire school devoted to the teaching of English as a second language. We may have been given inservice on the remediation of nonstandard English. It is more typical, however, to find a sprinkling of students in a school or class who require instruction in basic American English. Eager to learn, intent on making a good life for themselves, these students need our guidance. But how can we help them? How is it possible to manage the typical teacher's routine, solving every problem from loose teeth to paper grading, and still find the time to deal with the intricacies of teaching English to a non-native or speaker of nonstandard dialect? It seems we have learned nothing since those days in the late 1800s when my grandfathers started school.

Or have we? Contained herein are some classroom practices that show that we have indeed begun to gain some understanding of the many-faceted problem of bringing the non-native and the speaker of nonstandard dialect into the American mosaic.

1 The Teacher and the Non-native Student

Functional Lesson for ESOL Students

Dennise M. Bartelo
Spaulding High School, Rochester, New Hampshire

As a reading specialist and teacher of an adult class of English for speakers of other languages (ESOL), I have often found myself frustrated by the lack of quality materials for second language instruction. Many of the materials incorporate too many skills, use "Dick-Jane" sentence patterns, and focus on only one aspect of the total communication process of listening, speaking, reading, and writing. Although many materials for beginning reading instruction can be used, it is very difficult to find secondary level and adult materials that will bring real-life situations into the classroom and fit into limited ESOL school budgets.

In response to this situation, I have developed lessons integrating pronunciation, grammar, reading, and writing practice using functional materials within my community—the newspaper, restaurant menus, train and bus schedules, telephone books, and so on. For those teachers who have found themselves in the same position, I would like to share one of my lessons used successfully with my ESOL students on the topic of filling out a form.

Unit of Instruction—Personal Data

Objectives

1. Students will become aware of the basic questions used on simple forms.
2. Students will practice the simple present-tense question pattern, using the contraction *what's.*
3. Students will recognize and demonstrate usage of the contraction *what's* in a dialogue situation.

Content Item

Job forms.

Materials Used

Sample forms, pictures of various situations that utilize forms, flashcards of survival words used on forms, and a dialogue.

Activities for the Main Lesson

Teacher asks students to think about any forms they might have filled out in the past week. For example: Name the form you might have to fill out to pay for your groceries at the supermarket (a check cashing form). The teacher will elicit other responses: forms filled out to enroll in the class, forms for obtaining a passport or visa, driver's license forms, voting forms, credit card applications. The teacher will then point out that all of these forms ask personal information about a person in similar ways.

1. The teacher will direct the students' attention to sample forms, such as a charge account, and explain that it is important to fill out these forms correctly to get results, such as obtaining an account or getting a job.

2. The teacher will use flashcards to review the basic terms used on forms, such as name, address, references, and position, asking students to pronounce the word and relate to the class the meaning.

3. The teacher will draw an example of a sample form on the board (see below), and review each line, pointing to the word *last* and saying that this means, "What's your last name?"

(Last)	(First)	(Middle Initial)
(Address)		(ZIP Code)
(Telephone)		(Position Desired)

4. The teacher will point out that the short way to say "what is" is through the contraction *what's*. The use of the apostrophe is pointed out, the spelling, and the term used to describe this shortened form, *contraction*.

5. Students then are presented the dialogue below, with the teacher reading the entire thing through once, then asking the

students to repeat it line by line, and moving to the pace of four lines at a time, noting the intonation and pronunciation of the contraction pattern. The students can use the sample form as an aid, reinforcing the comprehension of form questions.

> If Forms Could Talk
>
> What's your first name?
>   What's your last?
> What is your middle initial?
>   Have you worked in the past?
>
> What is your address?
>   What's your zip code?
> What's the town you live in?
>   Have you a telephone?
>
> What's the name of your last boss?
>   What's the position you desire?
> What's the name of a close reference?
>   Have you ever been fired?

6. Students are then presented with a series of *what's* pattern questions and are asked to write these questions (which can be on a chart, sentence strip, or blackboard), matching the question to the situation it indicates.

   > *What's the date?* (Show students a calendar, giving them a clue to the task and reinforcing the usefulness of the drill.)
   >
   > *What's the price? What's the time? What's the weather?* (For each situation, the student should be able to see the functional item that matches the question. The teacher can use the newspaper, a calendar, and a grocery ad for sources of reference.)

7. Students are then assigned the sample form for homework, and are asked to fill it in and try to come to class with other *what's* pattern questions. (For example, What's the homework?)

Lesson Follow-up

More practice can be given on form completion and questions involved in an interview for a job.

Teaching a Few ESL Students in a Regular English Class

Alice V. Bulos
Palo Alto Unified School District, California

This article describes a program that will improve the English language skills of non-native students assigned to a regular English class at the middle school level. It is a program that is manageable; its goals are attainable, and it revolves around two requirements: first, that the teacher takes time to interview the non-native students, to determine their level of need, and second, that the teacher sets up, in a corner of the room, an ESL center or table with materials obtained from the district's instructional materials center, the speech and language department, the ESL or bilingual department, from his or her own resources, or from those of regular students.

This writer is aware that the readers of this article are probably teaching five classes, possibly 140 students, whose primary language is English and who are also at different levels of proficiency in understanding, speaking, reading, and writing skills. That, incidentally, is the progression of language acquisition: listening, listening with understanding, speaking, reading, and lastly, writing. The majority in the class has had almost five years to test their listening and speaking skills prior to entry into the nation's public school system. Do not expect to perform miracles with the non-native students. Language acquisition takes time; you can only hope to accelerate the progress through structured lessons that will supplement the language learning and cultural transfer which the non-natives are exposed to in the long hours that they are away from their homes. Your burden is a shared one.

Unless the non-natives are near the proficiency level, it is unrealistic to assume that they can keep up with your English course content while they are developing English language skills. Decide early whether you plan to grade them on their progress from point A to point B, or give them an F because they do not (can not) meet the standards for the class. Perhaps you want to enter into a brief, written contract with your supervisor in this matter. Enough said for theory and grading problems.

Interviewing Non-native Students

If the student (aged 11–14) speaks no English you'll need an interpreter. Contact the principal, who will have a list of all students in the school whose home language is other than English and can quickly tell you if there's another student or parent who speaks English plus the language of the student with whom you are trying to communicate. In other words, your principal can give you the name and phone number of a student or adult in the school (and with slightly more effort, the whole district) who can interpret for you. Take the time to hold a conference with the interpreter present. It will set up your ESL plans for the school year and give you a friend to assist you in reporting matters. The inventory of questions asked the student, or the student through an interpreter, should include the following:

An Inventory for Non-native Students

School _____ Today's date _____

Student's name _____ Age _____
            (last,   first)

Current grade assigned _____

1. Language spoken most frequently by student? _____
2. Alphabet different from English? _____
                       (yes, no)
3. Level of formal school actually completed? _____
4. Attended school in the last six months? _____
5. Can student read and write in native language? _____
6. Would student describe self as a poor, good, or excellent student in the home country? _____
7. Is student a visitor or planning to remain permanently in the United States? _____ If visiting, for how long? _____
8. As you observe the student, check one of the following:
    no English _____ limited, hesitant English _____
    broken English _____
9. Make a professional judgment about the student's motivation for academic work. (It may be months before you have objective evidence.) _____

Establishing Goals

Now, on a 4 × 6 index card, jot down at least four goals for that student in your class. For example, the goals that you write for a *non*-English-speaking student might include the following:

1. Teach survival phrases: "I'm sick," "Excuse me," "Stop!" and name, address, and phone number, and so on.
2. Teach the names of objects in your classroom (book, window, desk).
3. Teach the personal pronouns for the various forms of the verb *to be.*
4. Teach thirty regular verbs and twenty irregular verbs in the present progressive (*-ing* form).
5. Teach the days of the week, months, time expressions, and cardinal and ordinal numbers.

The goals that you write for a *limited*-English speaking student might include the following:

1. Review the present progressive form of forty regular and thirty irregular verbs.
2. Teach the simple past tense of the verbs, and the future tense using *going to* plus the present: "I'm going to swim."
3. Teach the alphabet and sounds.
4. Teach the adverbs of time, using the classroom calendar and clock.
5. Expose the student to ten new vocabulary words each day.

Having completed the interview(s) and written some simple goals, set about obtaining the resources you'll need for the year—for those materials in the hands of human resources (your other students) are going to be responsible for teaching the non-native students to speak English. Many of your students have had direct experience in watching their younger siblings or nephews and nieces, or the baby next door, learn to speak. Just as the Japanese emperor in the TV series *Shogun* said that the islanders were responsible for teaching Chamberlain to speak Japanese in six months, or die with him, so you too must enlist the aid of your students in this experiment in living together in a classroom for forty-five minutes every day for thirty-six school weeks. Your students will begin to examine the English language and to learn more about language in the process. Assign a different student each school week to be responsible for the ESL materials (set out on a corner table), and for listening to and speaking softly and distinctly to the ESL student(s).

The ESL Corner

Obtain materials from your instructional materials center, from primary and elementary school teachers in your district, or from the principal of an elementary school. Ask for cassettes of simple stories or simple songs that are short and can be recalled and re-told simply. Request penmanship books—both printed and cursive letters, grade 4 on downward—and old phonics books that have simple, colorful pictures in them. Get a cassette tape recorder and headset from your principal and install it at the ESL center. Bring a calendar, an old clock, some paper dolls, and simple games from home. Ask students to cut out magazine pictures and print on them the names of the objects, using sports, clothes, and other objects of particular interest to themselves and others of their age. Enlist students to cut tag board and neatly label everything in the room: the shades, the chalkboard, the closet, and so on. Borrow picture dictionaries—Richard Scarry's, for example—to help teach vocabulary. Buy or otherwise obtain a copy of Boggs's and Dixson's *English Step by Step with Pictures* (Regents Publishing Co., 1980), to use as a simplified guide for more structured lessons after extensive listening, listening with comprehension, and survival speaking skills have been achieved. Addison-Wesley's *New Horizon* series (levels 1 and 2) is appropriate for middle school students and has cassette tapes to accompany each book. The student who reads English well and "wants" to learn grammar can be put to work on Blumenthal's *Programmed English 2200* (Harcourt, Brace, Jovanovich, 1981), with little effort on the part of the teacher. Each ESL student should have a folder at the ESL classroom learning center and a composition book in which to record new vocabulary words.

Training your English students to help at the ESL table takes little time. Free them to use their imaginations. The calendar becomes a way to teach yesterday, today, tomorrow, this weekend, next weekend, last weekend, the day before yesterday, and many, many other useful expressions, as well as ordinal and cardinal numbers. The clock, and the pictures that the students have brought in, will generate ideas, vocabulary, and conversation about time, sports, clothes, and so on. Games will teach expressions, such as "It's your turn," "It's mine," and "It's a tie game." Dominoes, checkers, Bingo, and Old Maid are all fun and helpful in teaching beginning language.

Remind yourself occasionally that second language acquisition, when based on a strong first language foundation and literacy in the first language, can be accelerated, and that the four steps of listening, speaking, reading, and writing can, to some extent, occur simultaneously. The students will move at their own pace. On the other hand, if the students lack a strong language foundation on which to build, or have had sporadic educational experiences due to political havoc, the transfer from their native languages to English may take longer. The procedure is the same, but the teacher and the students must be patient. Such students will need to spend more time "just listening" in the beginning.

Having interviewed the students, jotted down a few realistic goals, set up an ESL corner, obtained materials, and set up a buddy system in the class, turn to your main job: teaching the other twenty-seven students English. You've already shown them how to be human.

Steps to Second Language Development in the Regular Classroom

Judith Walker de Félix
University of Houston

With worldwide migration at an all-time high, teachers in almost every country are having to cope with students who do not speak the language the teachers are supposed to be teaching. In the United States the situation is particularly acute, not only because of the large number of different languages represented in the public schools but also because of the unrealistic tradition of monolingual education in this country.

Teachers have seldom been prepared to develop the English skills of non-natives. They likewise can recall few role models in their own education. Their closest experience may have been a foreign language class they can attempt to model. However, most of them remember an almost magical routine of dialogs, pattern drills, and translation exercises—all of which seldom led to language proficiency. How are they supposed to create this magic, especially when the teachers do not speak Spanish, Farsi, and Vietnamese?

A language arts approach (LAA) to developing English skills in non-natives is the answer proposed by Gloria Sampson (1977). I have used the approach equally well in English-as-a-second-language (ESL) classes in Venezuela and in bilingual and regular classrooms in this country. Teachers I have trained in the LAA report that it is a reasonable approach which builds on their own strengths.

The Theory of LAA

Sampson (1977) describes the LAA as adapting strategies used in native language arts classes to ESL situations. She outlines four basic practices in LAA which should serve as the basis of ESL teaching: (1) fluency precedes accuracy; (2) rather than linguistic

11

structures being sequentially ordered, students will learn concepts and structures when they are ready for them; (3) instead of being just a model of appropriately spoken English, the teacher organizes successively more challenging tasks for the students; and (4) the acquisition of the linguistic function precedes the acquisition of the form.

The LAA is attractive to regular classroom teachers for several reasons. First, it builds on what good teachers already do well: develop skills in the English language. The only ESL methods they must learn include slowing down the pace for limited-English-speaking-ability (LESA) students, introducing phonics only after students have increased their vocabulary, building on native language whenever possible, understanding the nature of language strategies or function, and keeping informed of new strategies they may add to their repertoire.

From Theory to Practice

To put these ideas into practice, I recommend the following steps:

Step I: Develop Comprehension

All meaningful language must be preceded by cognition (Piaget, 1969). Teachers need to use a wide variety of resources to help students understand the concepts behind the language to be taught. Parents and other community resources, school personnel, pantomime, peer tutors, and native language materials are some suggested resources to use when developing understanding.

When parents are teaching babies to talk, they focus on understanding rather than trying to teach speaking. They stay in the here and now, avoiding abstract topics (Newport, et al., 1977). By using the same techniques, teachers can introduce concrete topics they can demonstrate with actions or pictures rather than trying to explain abstract notions in a language the student does not understand.

Step II: Select and Analyze Resource

All teachers are given prescribed books and other materials, some of which can be used for LESA students to help integrate them into the classwork. The materials will, of course, need to be adapted wisely. To do this the teacher must analyze the lesson for vocabulary, grammar, and linguistic function.

Vocabulary can be taught either for passive understanding or for active use. Concrete vocabulary should be taught for active use by categories. For instance, if the selected lesson has the word *meat*, the teacher should take advantage of the lesson to teach a variety of foods: different kinds of meats, most common foods served in the lunchroom, or sample foods from the four nutritional groups.

The presentation of the lesson should be as concrete as possible. Bringing bitesized pieces of meat would be most effective; pictures are second best. Vocabulary can easily be taught by a community, school, or peer aide. The peer can even follow up the lesson in the cafeteria.

Abstract vocabulary should seldom be taught for active use in the initial stages. Relying on dictionaries or other bilingual resources gives the best results, and these should be reserved for older students.

Grammar is likewise taught by categories so that students can begin to get an idea of the patterns in English structure. Traditional grammar rules should be avoided until the student is fluent because such rules frequently prevent communication of ideas. Language learners can become overwhelmed by grammar rules, which they see as details. Students would rather get their ideas across and not concern themselves with subject-verb agreement or correct tense (Wong-Fillmore, 1979).

Teachers can help students construct sentences by using pocket charts, flannel boards or other visual aids on which they can show where the vocabulary fits in a sentence. To continue with the example of *meat*, students can construct sentences like the following:

I (don't) like meat.
(Also: I like ham, etc.)
We had meat for lunch.
Meat is good.
Beef and ham are meat.

By selecting two or three types of sentences found in the lesson, the teacher can extend the students' structural repertoire.

Linguistic functions are more difficult to select from the lesson material because language use is more abstract than vocabulary or grammar. Nonetheless, no language can be logically studied without simultaneously studying how it is intended and how it is perceived.

Sampson (1977) highlights the following functions:

1. *Acknowledgement of self or other person.* In this function students need to be taught how to assert themselves, identify their interests, and recognize those of others. Many school materials describe children justifying their actions or identifying their needs. The teacher or peers can help students learn phrases to maintain their own interests and relate to others, such as "How do you feel about this?" "I need some help with my lesson." "May I please be excused?"

2. *Direct function.* Teachers frequently monitor actions in the classroom with this strategy. Students must understand what is required of them, so phrases such as "Work alone" and "Turn to page thirty-two" should be demonstrated to the English learner.

    Students, likewise, need to be able to use this function to collaborate with their peers and to plan actions.

3. *Interpretive function.* This function is one of the most common in classrooms. Students, especially those coming from other societies, need to be taught how to identify elements, recognize sequences, relationships, and causes. There are appropriate phrases used in the classroom that teachers and peers can teach the LESA student.

4. *Predictive function.* This strategy is also vital for producing good school work. Students ought to be given the phrases that allow them to forecast, hypothesize, anticipate consequences, recognize problems, and predict solutions. Continuing the previous example, students can be asked what kinds of meat they anticipate being served in the cafeteria. After learning about the nutritional qualities of meat, students can hypothesize about the nutritional consequences of vegetarianism.

5. *Imaginative function.* In this function material is renamed or a scene is built up through language. Students can describe what they might do if they had to fix dinner and there was no meat to prepare.

6. *Empathetic function.* This strategy is an excellent device for teachers to require students to perform because it includes role-playing. Learning a new language involves taking risks. To hide behind characters, particularly using puppets or masks, allows students a chance to perform without worrying about sounding off or making mistakes.

7. *Linguistic play function.* Songs and games are in this category. Having fun with language is a technique good language arts teachers have always stressed, and it helps relieve some of the pressure for LESA students.

Step III: Plan Activities according to the Students' Needs

Once the teacher has analyzed the lesson to be presented and has decided on the vocabulary, structure, and linguistic functions to be taught, he or she plans the activities to meet the students' needs. The students' age, cultural background, amount of English, amount and nature of home language education, and other personal factors should be taken into account so that the lessons are meaningful.

Step IV: Present Lesson from Known to Unknown

As with all teaching, the lessons must build on what the students know. The teacher, aide, or peer ascertains that the students comprehend the topic to be covered and then presents the content as concretely as possible.

As Sampson (1977) noted, the students may not acquire the new language as logically as expected in many ESL methodologies; they will retain only what they can use immediately. The teacher, nonetheless, attempts to present new information only on the basis of prior knowledge and comprehension of the concepts to be acquired.

Step V: Integrate and Reaffirm Skills

More language will be retained if students can integrate each concept into their personal lives and other school content areas. Teachers in self-contained classrooms can be sure to integrate the concepts into other content areas they teach and then affirm the skills in different contexts. When students meet with several teachers, those teachers should share their LAA lessons with their colleagues to be able to follow up other teachers' lessons in their own content area.

Although they may seem complex, these steps provide a sort of slow motion for the teacher. All these concepts are taught almost intuitively to native students as they progress through this society's school system. The only difficulty comes when teachers are asked to bring these strategies out in the open, often at a stage when the students' peers know them very well.

There are, however, several advantages to a multilingual classroom which these steps help elucidate. Children from various cultures may not have learned the school "rules" as they passed through the system. Helping teach a newcomer assists them to acquire more school savvy as they teach it.

Also monolingual students usually are not conscious of language use. An English learner in the classroom can help proficient speakers learn more about grammatical and functional manipulation. For instance, when teaching the newcomer about the self-assertion function, the teacher may ask all the students, "How do you get yourself invited for supper when your friend's mother is cooking your favorite meat?" As students exchange strategies, English learners are placed more in colloquial roles than they would be if they were isolated in a pullout ESL classroom, while the proficient speakers learn more about their own language use.

Although teachers are presented with challenges daily, few are as all-encompassing as having one or several students with whom they cannot communicate. By breaking the challenge down into feasible steps, perhaps these teachers can understand that they are not facing an overwhelming challenge.

References

Newport, E., et al., "Mother, I'd Rather Do It Myself: Some Effects and Noneffects of Maternal Speech Style," in C. Snow and C. Ferguson. *Talking to Children.* Cambridge: Cambridge University Press, 1977.

Piaget, J. *Psychologie et pedagogie.* Paris: Eds. Gonthier, 1969.

Sampson, G. P. "A Real Challenge to ESL Methodology," *TESOL Quarterly* 2, no. 3 (September 1977): 241–55.

Wong-Fillmore, Lily. "Individual Differences in Second Language Acquisition," in C. J. Fillmore, D. Kempler, and W. S-Y. Wang, *Individual Differences in Language Ability and Language Behavior.* New York: Academic Press, 1979.

Milk *o leche?*

Carlene Walker
University of Texas at El Paso

Advertisements, handbills, fast-food menus, signboards, and even grocery lists can help a non-English-speaking college student learn English.

Teaching my department's remedial English course, "Improving Reading and Writing Skills," I frequently find in class isolated students who speak only Spanish. One such student last summer was a middle-aged woman, born and educated in Mexico but long married to a successful Mexican-American businessman in this country. She had enrolled in the university, under our Open Admissions policy, after having seen her three children graduate from college. Only Spanish was spoken in her home because of her lack of English skills.

Although I required this student "to do her best" in regular classwork, I also used free materials to work with her in a personal program of "improving reading and writing skills." She cooperated fully in doing this extra work, which she handed in daily for my evaluation and then organized in her special notebook. As time permitted, she and I held short sessions in which she read her materials to me or talked to me about them—in English.

One assignment required her to cut out five illustrated advertisements, written in Spanish, from either the El Paso or the Juarez, Mexico, newspaper. Next, using the illustrations, she had to translate the ads into English. Another assignment sent her to find and copy five billboard signs written in Spanish and then translate them into English. On another occasion, she was required to start writing two grocery lists each time she went shopping, with one list being in English.

Fast-food menus, often written in both Spanish and English in our city, proved an effective learning aid. Giving my student an illustrated menu with the English lines masked, I insisted that

17

she write the English equivalent for each menu entry. A bilingual handbill advertising a *cumpleaños fiesta* (birthday party) promoted by a hamburger restaurant turned out to be an especially effective aid for both student and teacher.

Such "easy" practice with English led my student to feel more confident in her second language. That confidence increased her willingness and incentive to tackle more difficult regular assignments, so that she was able to pass the course with a minimum grade and return to college for a second semester.

I recommend this procedure for working with any student who may be able to read more English than he or she can speak. Non-English-speaking individuals, thanks to advertising and television, often have more practice in reading English than they or we realize.

For example, on even her first grocery list, my student reminded herself to buy milk, not *leche*, and Coors Light, not *cerveza*.

Starting Off a Non-native Student in a College Basic Skills Course

Robert W. Blake
SUNY College at Brockport

On the first day of Communication Skills 102, Francisco (not his real name) sits in the second row, smiling at me and at everybody around him. He is slender, and when he stands up at the end of class I see he is tall, close to six feet. He has curly brown hair, brown eyes, and a wispy mustache. I find out later that he had come to New York City a few years earlier from the Dominican Republic; he tells me this in a later narrative: "I came alone from Santo Domingo, where there is no winter; but warm sunshine weather. Like California, Santo Domingo was a day spent on the beach, relaxing and enjoying." For the last four years he has lived on FDR Drive along the East River in Manhattan, taking classes—again, as I learn later—in both Spanish and English. This is his first class in which the instruction is entirely in English. But here he is now at a small, upstate New York college in a climate and educational environment about as far removed from Santo Domingo weather and culture as he can get and still remain on earth. So on this bright September day Francisco sits, smiling, obviously eager to learn how to write English in this gringo classroom.

The communication skills course Francisco finds himself in is a remedial course for those students who—on the basis of past performance in high school—have been identified as not being ready to enter the first of the two regular college communication skills courses which all students must successfully complete before moving on to further collegiate work. Most of the twenty-five students in the class are native speakers of English. There is, however, another remedial course in communication skills each semester, Communication Skills 101, usually with two sections, for all students whose native language is something other than English. But frequently several of these foreign students overflow the two classes and the immigrants are placed in "regular" basic classes with instructors reputed to know something about teaching them how to write.

So how can I help Francisco—and two other Hispanics and one Egyptian as well—to write academic English? Should I be fluent in Spanish? It would be nice, I suppose, but I don't have any Spanish. I do, however, know some French and German and did live in Germany for a year and a half, during which time I traveled throughout Europe, making a strenuous attempt to assimilate the languages and cultures of people far different from me. Should I have special training in Teaching English to Speakers of Other Languages (TESOL is the acronym for this mouthful)? I don't, but I have taught writing at all school and college levels and have a fairly extensive knowledge of linguistics, including the grammar and phonology of English as well as the most basic notions from psycholinguistics and sociolinguistics. Most important, though, I consider myself sympathetic to the problems non-native speakers of English may have in learning how to write academic English. I go on at this length about my personal background because, contrary to what the vociferous advocates of bilingual education and TESOL hold, most English teachers in regular classrooms will find, possibly to their surprise, that their special professional training and experience have prepared them quite well to teach these new immigrants to America how to become competent writers—be they from the Dominican Republic, Puerto Rico, Viet Nam, Japan, or Egypt.

Given the present situation in the classroom and my particular training and experience, what's my first step in helping Francisco learn how to write English well enough to go on to the regular communication skills course? First, I must find out at this point simply how well he can write. To do this, I give him a two-part diagnostic test. Section A of Part II has ten sentences with common usage and basic punctuation errors. The students are directed to rewrite the sentences, in spaces provided on the test, correcting the errors as they go along. Section B contains ten common words and phrases, such as *your*, *there*, or *it's*, with directions to "write a sentence in which you use the word or phrase correctly." Section C addresses the skill of "combining groups of sentences by means of coordination and using proper indicators of coordination" by giving the students ten sets of simple sentences to combine. The last section of Part II deals with the skill of "combining sentences by means of subordination," directing the students to combine by subordination ten sets of simple sentences.

The second part of the diagnostic competency test—which is my chief concern within the scope of this paper—is a classroom writing assignment, leading to a piece of whole discourse and designed to ensure that "all students who intend to continue their studies at the college can complete several tasks which demonstrate knowledge and control of the writing process and the conventions of formal, written English."

In the written directions of the diagnostic essay, the students are told: "You will demonstrate competency in Part I if you can write a paragraph that (1) follows the directions carefully, (2) contains relevant examples, (3) has very few errors in spelling and punctuation, (4) includes appropriately developed sentences with clear transitions." Pretty hard reading for Francisco, I realize, but I read the directions aloud to the class—very slowly and distinctly—and answer all questions before he and the others proceed.

This is the writing assignment the students are given to complete in class within a full period. In devising this assignment, we wanted to make it specific and realistic with a clear description of the rhetorical elements of *purpose, audience,* and *writer's role* or *persona* the students must attend to:

> Directions: You have been asked to fill out a recommendation for a friend who has applied for a job as a clerk in a bank. One section of the form has these directions.
>
> Describe the way the applicant behaves when he/she is corrected, disagreed with, and/or given rather demanding instructions. Be sure to give specific examples of the behavior you describe.
>
> Write a one-paragraph entry of approximately 200 words. Be sure to include specific examples. Remember also that your skill in writing may have an effect on your friend's future employment.

What Francisco wrote in response to the assignment is reproduced in figure 1.

The next step is to analyze Francisco's paper and talk with him about what he needs to work on to become a better writer. Using a simple "Student Writing Analysis Sheet," I write comments in these categories: I. Rhetorical Task, II. Relation of Parts to Whole, III. Sentence Structure, IV. Word Choice, and V. Mechanics. Francisco's "Student Writing Analysis Sheet" is presented as figure 2.

So what can I say about Francisco's writing? It is of utmost importance that I am able to move past his serious problems with English sentences, diction, and mechanics to note two really significant aspects of his writing. First, from this piece, there is no

To whon may Concern:

The first thing that would like to write in these recomenendations form is. I know José Collado a ver long time. He is a excellent asset of his community, friends, and his family. I think there are not a easy way to describe the behaves of my friend Jose Collado when he is corrected by his friends or by any other person. Is it very inusual to human being acept the coretion by other person but José Callado do the opposity that we the human being does. He acept the coretion. And too no like to follow the open When he is doing some thing wrong. Let me give a example of how Jose act when is corr he had being corrected by ——— someone. We were wating Five month ago we were working together in Pawn toun grocery store. One day he was putting soda in the on the refrigerator, mk. Vallego. Luis Vallejo the ow owner of the grocery came. came and say to him "You are doing something wrong." Jose stop and says to me the MR. Vallego "What are doing wrong?" MR. Vallejo say "I won't tell you. Then Jose say if you don't correct me I will no continuening puntting soda in. finally MR. Luis says you has to put soda in stright line, more organiz." The end was that Jose follow the corection by MR. Vallejo and after that he was one of The only person in the store who could organize organize the Refigeratior better than MR. Vallejo. Finally, I strongly believe that if you hire José Collado he will be one more asset to yours bank.

Very truly your,

Figure 1. Francisco's paper.

Student Writing Analysis Sheet

Student _____ Francisco _____

Assignment ___ Recommendation for Bank Clerk's Job ___   Date _____

Category	Analysis	Recommendations
I. *Rhetorical Task* (understand directions, recognize rhetorical aim, use conventions of mode, consistent point of view, sense of audience)	You understand the directions well. You know your audience, and you keep your point of view consistent.	Good work. Keep it up!
II. *Relation of Parts to Whole* (organization or sequencing; generalizations supported by reasons, details, examples; appropriate level of generalization; coherence)	You have a clear sense of structure. Good use of examples. Dialogue makes the paper immediate. Good use of transitions. Good balance between specifics and general statement.	Again, good work. Keep it up.
III. *Sentence Structure* (varied sentence structures, free of sentence errors, neither short and choppy nor long and stringy sentences)	Major problems with English sentences. Problems with verbs.	Need concentrated and continuing work with "English" sentences, correct verb forms.
IV. *Word Choice* (clear, concrete rather than vague language; words used accurately; single words used for longer structures; mixture of levels, unconscious word repetition)	Pretty good use of English words but need to widen your English vocabulary.	Work needed on precise English words and on expanding your English vocabulary.
V. *Mechanics* (spelling, punctuation, capitalization, handwriting, format)	Problems with spelling, punctuation, capitalization, and handwriting.	Need drill on mechanics of written English. Practice in proofreading.

Figure 2. Analysis of Francisco's writing.

doubt that he understands well the rhetorical task he has been assigned—the purpose of his discourse. He also assesses correctly the audience for whom he is writing and assumes a writer's role (persona) appropriate to convey his message to this particular audience. I'm impressed by his ability to handle maturely these crucial aspects of effective writing. Second, he has a good sense of the structure of the piece; the paper has a definite beginning, middle, and ending. He balances generalizations with specific examples and also uses dialogue—albeit not always punctuated correctly—to enhance the piece. And he employs naturally and effectively transitional devices such as "first," "let me give you an example," and "finally." In several significant ways, he is an accomplished writer.

Now to Francisco's difficulties. I can see quite clearly that he has serious problems with written English sentences, but that is no surprise since he has been writing English, especially academic English, for only a few years. The way he puts his sentences together is simply not "English." This lack of the "feel" for how English sentences "go" is most evident in his inability to control the English verb system. "I know José Callado for very long time." "The owner of the store came and say to him. . . ." "José stop and says to me. . . ." "Mr. Vallejo say. . . ." He really doesn't have much trouble with diction—the precise use of words—but the problems he does have appear to stem from his lack of experience with English vocabulary. And finally, he has trouble with spelling, capitalization, punctuation, and even handwriting simply because he has not been writing academic English for very long. But even his spellings show a good phonetic sense of the sounds of the words. To his credit, he certainly is not afraid to use the words even though he's not completely sure of their spellings. I have no doubt he will become a better speller of English words as he writes a lot, learns how to proofread more carefully—with dictionary in hand— and learns some of the regularities and vagaries of English spelling.

Now that I have looked carefully at Francisco's writing, and talked to him about it, what do we do next? It is not within the scope of this paper to describe in detail the writing assignments, sentence combining activities, exercises in the mechanics of written English, and workshopping activities I planned for Francisco, but I can describe the general features of Francisco's program in the basic communication skills course.

1. The writing program for Francisco will be built upon my understanding of where he is at the beginning of the class.

I have available a piece of his writing and can see that in a mature and confident way he is able to handle key elements in academic writing. I can also see just as clearly that he has serious problems with English sentences. I realize, furthermore, that he is a "stranger in a strange land" who needs all the personal support and encouragement he can get, even more than native speakers of English deserve.

2. Francisco's writing program will be based on what I consider a natural sequence of writing activities. He will move from writing autobiography (an early memory) and biography (a "phase" biography of a close friend or relative) to several types of traditional exposition (use of examples and illustrations, comparison and contrast, cause and effect, and a "how to" or process essay). For me, such a sequence is logical for two reasons. First, with the initial narratives, Francisco will gain confidence in his writing ability by writing about events and people he knows well. Second, he will write narrative first—in which he can follow a natural, chronological structure —before he tackles exposition—in which he must create his own arbitrary and artificial structures. (See James Moffett's justification of this kind of scheme, especially in the chapter "Kinds and Orders of Discourse," in *Teaching the Universe of Discourse*, Houghton Mifflin, 1968).

3. For all writing assignments, Francisco will create complete pieces of discourse. Although he will do exercises in usage, sentence combining, and the mechanics of written English— to complement his writing of whole narratives and essays— he will not be taught to believe that such drill in mechanics is in fact writing. I can't emphasize this point strongly enough. Many English teachers, some of my colleagues included, believe that a program for students deficient in writing skills should include heavy doses of drill and workbook exercises, gradually leading to writing single sentences and, possibly toward the end of a course, short paragraphs. No instructional plan could be worse for any would-be writer, and it's especially harmful for a so-called basic writer like Francisco. Francisco will become a competent writer—not by filling in blanks, crossing out incorrect usage items, underlining subjects once and predicates twice, and by putting together banal paragraphs, but by actually producing complete pieces of writing for specific audiences.

4. While creating these whole pieces of discourse, Francisco will, time after time, cycle through the composing process. He will interact with his classmates and me in one-to-one conferences, in small groups, and with the class as a whole during the prewriting, revising, and editing stages of composing. During the drafting stage, of course, he must work alone, and he must come to terms with the idea that although the drafting stage is a frightening and solitary one, it is nevertheless a necessary one for composing. He needs to go through the process enough times so he will learn to profit from the feedback others can give him about his writing and will not be a stranger to this process when he tackles any writing task.

5. Francisco and I will talk about his writing at every stage, from early drafts to finished products, sometimes for a few minutes but periodically for much longer times. Although he gets feedback about his writing from others, it is essential that he hear from me—a more experienced, especially trained teacher of writing—in specific terms, what is admirable in his writing but just as specifically how he can continue to improve. Short, oral conferences with Francisco are far more useful than extensive red marks on his papers—without a personal conference—would be.

6. Francisco will complete extensive and frequent sentence combining activities, discuss them with his classmates, take quizzes on the activities, and attempt to use the new structures in his compositions. Such activities will help him become aware of the range of English sentences available to him.

7. Francisco will do many exercises on the mechanics of English —standard usage, punctuation, capitalization, spelling, and on other miscellaneous problems of written academic format —and will discuss them with his classmates, take quizzes on these matters, and, I trust, learn to handle correctly items from these categories in his papers. Although he and his classmates will be taught to be scrupulous in proofreading their compositions for mechanical errors, they will also benefit from short but frequent drills on such matters.

Essentially, Francisco's program for learning how to write academic English will involve as much writing and pointed, direct discussion of his writing with me and with his classmates as we can manage within a semester. I want him to feel confident about the process of writing a whole piece of discourse, and perhaps even somewhat more comfortable than he had been before with these exotic English sentences.

I have found out where Francisco is in the development of his ability to write academic English. He and I have a fairly accurate idea of what his strengths and weaknesses are. I have set up a comprehensive program, based on my background and experience and the best information available, for helping him to improve his writing.

Now for both of us the hard work begins.

Center for the Study of Language and Culture

Zenobia Verner
University of Houston

Patricia Williams
Sam Houston State University

With the current immigration situation and with large numbers of foreigners entering the country on a temporary basis, your chances for having one or more students in your middle or high school classes who speak little or no English are increasing. In most instances your school system will schedule such students into an ESL (English as a Second Language) course during one period of the day, but for the remainder of the day they will attend regular classes. Since they may be unable to benefit from most of your English instruction for lack of English language proficiency, you may wish to prepare a center in your classroom in which these students and any tutors you may have available may work.

Materials

Place junk mail, catalogs, magazines, newspapers, scissors, paste, glue, 3 × 5 cards, and paper in the language study center. If you have one available, the Language Master or comparable unit and blank cards will also be useful. Organize materials neatly in appropriate folders, boxes, or baskets on a table or shelves. For students who are literate in their home language, also furnish a dictionary in both English and the home language. (Students who have attended school only in the United States are unlikely to be literate in their home language.) In addition to the dictionary, furnish an introductory English book written in the home language. That book will describe such important items as sound symbol relationships, English word order in sentences, types of sentences, and it will answer other immediate questions the student may have. A few representative books are listed at the end of this article. Your librarian should be able to help you find any others you might need.

Activities

Students, depending on their level of English proficiency, can complete activities such as those given below. Plan to use a peer tutor whenever possible who can serve to bring the student into interaction with other class members whenever appropriate.

Vocabulary

Students can search catalogs and junk mail to prepare dictionaries. They soon become adept at finding words for catalog pictures: for example, a picture of a refrigerator and the word *refrigerator*. The use of a catalog enables students to seek out first those things which they wish to learn. For the least proficient, we recommend the use of 3 × 5 cards on which they place a picture on one side and the word on the reverse side, or Language Master cards with word and picture and a peer to record the pronunciation of the word. If no peers are available, they can use their home language dictionary to locate the word, or you or any student can use the Language Master to record the pronunciation. If students don't find material they want in a catalog, the Oxford picture dictionary may be of help. Students can use the resulting cards for practice alone or with peers.

As they gain proficiency, they can use a spiral or loose-leaf notebook and put several words, pictures, and some sentences of their own on each page. Items in the notebook need not be alphabetically arranged as they are in the dictionary. Rather they might be categorized in some other fashion. Some possibilities include having them find words and pictures for (1) a particular room in the home, (2) modes of transportation, (3) foods Americans eat for breakfast, lunch, and dinner, or (4) clothing for men and women.

As students gain proficiency in reading and speaking through ESL and your class, you can have them do different kinds of activities at the center, based on their needs, interests, and proficiency. Students can search for synonyms, antonyms, homonyms, and acronyms in materials provided. You still need to prepare examples of what you wish them to do. Usually it is productive to have them find one of a pair of the above and write the other. For example, they quickly find the word *sale* in junk mail or in the newspaper and may be able to write the word *sail*. Then they might write a sentence of their own and read it to another student.

They can search for words which they know but which are used in a context different from that which they know, such as *general* as a military title versus *general* merchandise.

They can select new words they wish to learn, look them up, and write sentences or collect pictures to help them remember them. At this stage they might select new words from junk mail, display ads, or other easy-to-read illustrated material.

Find out from the students or from their ESL teacher when they begin to work on specific word endings such as *-er* and *-er*, *-est* (as in *player*—one who plays, *higher, highest*), *-ing*, *-ed*, *-s*, *-es* (both nouns and verbs), and have them locate them in center materials. Similar work can be done with prefixes and suffixes.

You can give them a sentence in which they change the meaning at least ten times by changing the verb. For example, the sentence might read, "A man went down the street." Students find words in newspapers, magazines, or junk mail to replace *went*. They might substitute *ran, sauntered, picked his way, tiptoed, barreled, skipped, hopped*. You can leave any sentence slot open, or you can have them expand sentences.

Students can search for words that indicate direction, such as *up, down, around, right, left, east, above*.

Reading Comprehension

Students can search for words that signal sequence in directions (*first, then, next, finally*), and then move on to easy-to-read items where other, more difficult, clues must be used to determine sequence. Front-page newspaper items may contain time (2:30 a.m.), day (Tuesday), month (July), or other (last week). Sports pages include stories that depend on such words as *inning, half,* and *quarter* for determining sequence.

They can practice following written directions by selecting material from the center which requires them to fill in forms and paste on stickers.

They can select a newspaper article or junk mail item and then read and check to see if the headline tells the main idea or if it was designed mainly to get their attention. If they determine, for example, that it contained the main idea, they might try to write a headline of another type—one that would attract attention.

Students can attempt to answer simple questions about junk mail and newspaper articles or magazine advertisements. What are they trying to sell? Who is the article about? Where does the action take place? When did it happen? What does it cost?

All kinds of activities can involve classification of material and information—things the students like versus things they don't like—fruit, vegetables, meats. Classification activities can be combined with forming sensory impressions by having students find and classify things they can see, feel, hear, taste, smell.

Searches for main ideas lead them into all types of language learning center materials. Your regular students usually need practice in finding main ideas and enjoy assisting your second language students in this search.

Reading part of an article or looking at a picture can lead to their predicting outcomes. Again, involve your regular students and let each list as many possible outcomes as they can and compare their lists. Students can write their own endings and read them to each other. They can discuss implications of the various alternatives they listed: What if___? Then ___ .

Students can speculate about the author's purpose in writing various types of material—newspaper column, junk mail letter, letter to the editor, magazine article.

Possibilities for using your center materials for reinforcing or practicing reading skills are endless. Simply look at your skills and prepare activities similar to those in textbooks, yet use your center materials for the reading. Just be sure to prepare activities for a variety of skills rather than falling into the trap of working on only a few with major focus on locating and remembering details in what is read.

Oral Language

Be sure your students share work done at the center with peers. They can read their words, sentences, and other papers they have written to other students. They can talk about the main ideas they found, author's purpose, things they like and don't like. Everything they do furnishes opportunity for talking, reading aloud, and trying to communicate with others. Be sure you encourage them to experiment with the language through interaction with you and with other students.

You can select and record several short items from materials in the center. Have students listen and note the length of your pauses at commas, periods, and other marks of punctuation. They can follow up by reading something themselves and having you or a student listen to see if their oral punctuation is appropriate.

Students may ask you or another student to record a selection that is of special interest to them. This furnishes opportunity for study of pronunciation, promotes vocabulary development, and develops their listening skills.

Regular Students

Don't overlook the opportunity to use your center for your regular students also. It furnishes students a chance to look at persuasive techniques used in advertising and politics. In addition, they can use it as resource material for their own persuasive writing. Endless opportunities exist for practicing almost every reading and thinking skill. Listed at the end of this article are some student materials designed for use with newspapers that can be used with junk mail with intermediate and advanced ESL, as well as with other students who need to improve reading skills.

Junk mail, catalogs, newspapers, and magazines are particularly appropriate for use with students of varying levels of English reading proficiency. If students are free to select their own materials, they tend to choose only those that are meaningful to them and with which they can experience some success in reading. In addition, students from other cultures learn much about American culture through such material, and they like it because it frequently focuses on events and things which they recognize in their new environment.

Resources

Bergman, Peter M. *The Basic English-Chinese, Chinese-English Dictionary.* New York: New American Library, 1980.

Culhane, Terry, and Jean Pierre Chandler. *English Alone: A Self-Instructional Course for French Speakers.* Elmsford, N.Y.: Maxwell House, Pergamon Press, 1981.

Graham, Carolyn. *Jazz Chants for Children* (with cassette). London: Oxford University Press, 1979.

Leba, John. *Everyday English for Vietnamese Learners* (with cassettes). Houston: Zieleks, 1976.

Nguyen Hy Quang. *English-Vietnamese Phrasebook with Useful Word List for Vietnamese Speakers.* Washington, D.C.: Center for Applied Linguistics, 1975.

Mustelier, Leonel. *English-Spanish (Cuban) Phrasebook with Useful Word List.* Washington, D.C.: Center for Applied Linguistics, 1981.

Parnwell, E.D. *Oxford Picture Dictionary of American English: English Monolingual Edition.* London: Oxford University Press, 1979.

Parnwell, E.D. *Oxford Picture Dictionary of American English: English/ French Edition.* London: Oxford University Press, 1979.

Parnwell, E.D. *Oxford Picture Dictionary of American English: English/ Spanish Edition.* London: Oxford University Press, 1979.

Parnwell, E.D. *Oxford Picture Dictionary of American English: English/ Japanese Edition.* London: Oxford University Press, 1981.

Verner, Zenobia. *Collections: A Newsbook of Vocabulary Activities.* Houston: Clayton, 1979.

Verner, Zenobia. *Newsbook of Capitalization Activities and Games.* Houston: Clayton, 1979.

Verner, Zenobia. *Newsbook of Reading Comprehension Activities.* Houston: Clayton, 1978.

2 Peer Teaching

Storytelling: A Way to Teach Non-native Students

Susan J. Berthouex
Crestwood School, Madison, Wisconsin

Robin S. Chapman
University of Wisconsin, Madison

"Kathunori Tretes bird fly." This was the first story that my non-English-speaking Japanese student told in my first grade class at the Surabaya International School, Indonesia. It was also the first story he read.

In that class were fourteen children. Two of the children were native English speakers, ten spoke English as a second language with varying degrees of skill. Two children, one of whom was Kathunori, knew no English on the first day of school. All were to be instructed in English.

Storytelling was the method I chose for integrating Kathunori into the group, teaching English as a spoken language, and teaching reading. This article is about Kathunori's progress in learning to speak and read English through his own stories. I believe that the storytelling method can also be useful in American classrooms for teachers who must help their own Kathunoris—the one or two children from different cultures with no skills in English—who must be taught with all the others.

The Storytelling Method

Every morning each child in the class was invited to join me at the typewriter and tell me a story, which I would type exactly as it was dictated. During the first two weeks Kathunori did not participate, although he often observed attentively as other children told stories. The third week, he was eager to tell about a bird he had seen in the mountains. *Fly* was not in his vocabulary but he had learned *bird*. Saying his name, the name of the town, *bird*, and

37

flapping his arms, he then brought the word *fly* into his English vocabulary and into his first story:

> Kathunori Tretes bird fly.

We laughed and he flapped his arms and said "fly" several times during the day as he showed others his story—a joyful first.

Kathunori received the typewritten copy for his own book of stories. I also made a carbon copy for my file. It is from these files that the boy's progress is recorded.

Kathunori's Progress

One of Kathunori's stories from the first weeks of school was:

> Ship is in the water.
> Ship is big.
> Truck in the ship.
> Go to Bali. My ship like.

He was telling about crossing on a ferry from the island of Java to the island of Bali. The ferry carried his family and their van.

Another day, Kathunori described the airplanes flying over his house:

> The airplane is fly.
> The airplane flies near my house.
> It is loud.
> My look.

It is evident from these stories that Kathunori developed English vocabulary rapidly. Also evident is his far slower mastery of English syntax. Like any small child learning to speak English as a first language, he made many mistakes. His mistakes reflected interference from his own first language as well as his very limited English skills. But his eagerness to try was the spirit I wanted. And so the stories were typed exactly as he spoke them, allowing him to talk freely and read more easily.

Kathunori's opportunities to learn English occurred only at school; at home he spoke Japanese and in his neighborhood he spoke Indonesian. He learned English primarily from his classmates. There were two places in school where talking was encouraged: on the playground and in the activity centers that filled the morning. I set up these centers especially to create interaction. Math, science, and prereading activities were set up for pairs or threesomes to share materials. The children had to talk to each other to get the colors needed for painting, the scissors and paste for construction, or a turn at working the puzzle. As the semester progressed, the projects became collaborative, requiring joint planning and discussion: jump-rope counting rhymes, a classroom mural, measuring shadows at different times of day. Two hours a week of small-group instruction in English as a second language were provided by the ESL teacher.

The storytelling time was thus not the only opportunity Kathunori had for learning and using English, but it was a time during which he enjoyed using his new skills. By the second month he was telling stories every other day. His vocabulary expanded even as his inadequate syntax lagged behind:

> Kenya many many lions.
> Lions is eating the zebra and the buffalo.
> Maiween, Japanese boy, in Kenya.
> Kenya is zebra many many.
> Lion is eating zebra not many.

The length of Kathunori's stories increased from an average of four sentences per story in September to eight in October to eleven in November. The average utterance length remained constant at about 4.3. Here, for example, is the story he told on November 30 about playing baseball soccer:

> My school ground play kick base.
> My Satosi say "You pitcher."
> My no like pitcher.
> My many pitcher.
> Satosi say "Monday, Uichi and Satosi pitcher."
> Satosi not like pitching.
> Satosi not good kicking.
> My throw. Satosi kick ball.
> Satosi running stop first base.
> Uichi kicking third.
> Uichi is many second base.
> Uichi big hit.
> Satosi running home in.
> Uichi third base.
> Satosi big kick.
> Uichi home in.
> Satosi is second base.
> Uichi is running my throw.
> He out.
> Uichi say, "Not out."
> Uichi second base.
> Satosi kicking.
> My not kick base.

Satosi no play kick base.
Satosi is in second classroom.
And Uichi is in classroom.
My kick base looking.
Cachino say, "Not Satosi team."
My say, " Satosi team."
My talking Cachino.
Bell ring.
Cachino and my in classroom.
Cachino gives sports car eraser Joo Hyon.
Joo Hyon is give candy Cachino.
My say, "Give bubble gum."
Joo Hyon say, "Give sports car eraser."

In those three months, Kathunori returned to the same topics only twice. Every day was a new story. He talked about his family, boats, airplanes, various animals (including crocodiles, birds, lions, cheetahs, elephants, bears, fish, gorillas, orangutans, alligators, turtles, and beavers), games (including foursquare, horse, bowling, soccer, and kickball), money, places that he visited, a Japanese whaling ship, and Japanese school.

Kathunori's first-semester progress was in vocabulary and elaboration of his plots. His ability to put what he wanted to say into standard English sentence structure continued to be rudimentary, and I sometimes wondered if I had done him a disservice by accepting his limited attempts at English. But I knew that mothers readily accept whatever pronunciation and sentence structure their own children use when they are learning to talk. They correct their children for using the wrong words but not the wrong grammar. Kathunori was enthusiastic about his storytelling and eager to interact with the English-speaking children in class. And so I continued to transcribe his stories as he told them.

In December other children began to join Kathunori in his storytelling. I welcomed the group stories because they created opportunities for listening as well as storytelling. Each child inspired the others to new heights (or depths). From that time on Kathunori seldom told stories alone.

Many of Kathunori's early topics had been drawn from life. His stories about animals were an exception. They were forerunners of a series I remember as the Jungle Stories. Threat—and escape from threat—was their common theme. The topic was so powerfully attractive to the listening children that the plot was copied with variations by almost all members of the class. The first of these stories with a jungle setting occurred in February. Kathunori and Joo Hyon collaborated on it, introducing their classmates as characters. Here is a fragment of Kathunori's portion:

> Cachino no go jungles and Thomas he not go jungle and Garry he want go jungle and he cannot go jungle. And he want touching tiger and lion and all animals. And today go with Joo Hyon, Thomas and Dinyar and Jimmy and he go Sumatran jungles. Garry he catching monkeys and tigers and lions. And Joo Hyon he catching all animals. And Thomas is not by snake. He want it Thomas and Dinyar. Dinyar run away. Dinyar cry, "Help! Help!" like that. And Joo Hyon he did not die. Thomas and Dinyar and Jimmy and Garry is he come back. And my and Joo Hyon catching all animals.

The jungle stories provided children with a basic fantasy plot to repeat, elaborate, and vary. They listened with increased interest and attention to their friends' stories. Its familiar framework allowed Kathunori to learn and experiment with basic sentence patterns. For example, the children would list who went to the jungle and who didn't, who was hurt or threatened by what, and how they responded. They developed basic sentence patterns to express this information, substituting characters and events to suit their fancy. Thus the Jungle Stories took on the character of pattern practice drills, with an important difference: The children had a purpose in the construction of these sentences.

In the last third of the year Kathunori's stories averaged thirty sentences. The number of words per sentence had increased to 5.7. He was saying more in each sentence and contributing more sentences. Here is an example from April.

> Dinyar go to the jungle and Dinyar have a lion.
> And the Dinyar go to Japan and King Kong go to Japan too.
> And Dinyar go to the zoo and him in lion house.
> And lion bite Dinyar.
> And Dinyar bite lion neck.
> Tiger bite Dinyar and Dinyar bite tiger neck.
> He see elephant and elephant see Dinyar.
> Dinyar he want throw a elephant.
> And King cannot throw an elephant. And broken bones.
> And Dinyar say, "Ouch, ouch, ouch!"
> And again go to the Japanese zoo.
> There have not house.
> He not Japanese have like that at zoo like a bus.
> And look at animals.
> Dinyar not ride bus.
> And Dinyar go in the zoo.
> And lion bite a neck and Dinyar bite a lion neck.

And him bite a thigh.
And him bite a head.
And lion say, "Ouch! Ouch! Ouch!"
And Dinyar again come a zoo and elephant saw a lion and lion
    say "Ouch!" And in the water.
And him die.

In this story, Kathunori understood, relished, and played with English word order: When the tiger bit Dinyar, Dinyar bit the tiger. His correct use of word order contrasted markedly with his stories of the fall. Finally, he was mastering basic English sentence patterns.

Storytelling and Reading

What about learning to read? Kathunori's reading materials for the year were the stories he told. In class he would choose a line or two that he wished to copy for writing practice. He might also illustrate the sentence. The typewritten stories, illustrations, and his printed copies were stapled into booklets that Kathunori shared with his friends and family. He practiced reading from the booklets to me, an aide, or small groups.

The aide tested Kathunori's word recognition by underlining words he chose from his own stories when he could say them correctly. Three underlinings on separate days meant he could have the word on a card. These word cards were used for independent writing, to practice individually or with a friend, or to teach a friend some new words. The children valued these cards as tangible evidence of achievement.

Kathunori began accumulating word cards in late November, two months after he began telling stories. By the end of the fall semester he had forty-one cards. He added eighty more in the first three months of the spring semester.

Lessons for American Classrooms

Few teachers in American classrooms will have the advantages that Kathunori and I had of small class size, although most can find volunteer typists. Nor will there necessarily be the extra time in the English-as-a-second-language classroom that Kathunori had, or the easy acceptance of each other that my multilingual, multicultural students offered. But most teachers will want, as I did, to include the non-English-speaking in as much regular classroom activity as possible. And all will hope that the experience can contribute to the child's social integration, communication skills in English, and reading and writing skills.

My experience in teaching Kathunori and the other children of the Surabayan classroom leads me to two conclusions about the storytelling method. First, it allows the teacher to create an environment in which the child wants to communicate in English, it has many opportunities to do so, and it is almost always success-ful. The typewritten stories provide a tangible record of that success. The stories that are told become a focus for further inter-action. Children listen to each other and begin to collaborate in telling their stories. They copy, parody, and elaborate upon each other's stories. They value and attend to each other's communica-tion. The stories become a shared topic of conversation.

Second, the storytelling method allows the teacher to provide a context in which written English can be learned by a child with very limited vocabulary. The child learns to read and write the words she or he can already say about topics of the child's own choice.

Because the stories are the child's own, she or he can predict both general content and specific words. Interest is high, success is frequent. Reading in English does not have to wait until the spoken language is mastered. The storytelling method creates the child's own reading program, exactly matched to his or her current interests and English skills. The child's first story requires only a handful of words: "Kathunori Tretes bird fly."

Group Activities for Non-native Students in Regular Freshman English

Marsha Z. Cummins
Bronx Community College, CUNY

Dividing a class into small groups of four or five students whose tasks are to discuss a subject and then write the results of their group effort has been a strategy that I find extremely effective in integrating the non-native students into a regular freshman English composition classroom. The small groups continue to meet with the same members throughout the semester, and their writing is always presented to the entire class. This system gives continuity and increasing security to the non-native students while also providing a larger audience—the class as a whole.

Non-native students in our community college have taken ESL courses before they enter the freshman English course. This experience provides them with instruction in written and spoken English and a model of spoken English in the form of the instructor and tapes. However, the ESL student lacks the opportunity for spoken communication with native students, an essential element in learning idioms, syntax, and pronunciation because it allows the non-native to practice by imitating and it provides instant feedback. Non-native students are frustrated by this lack of opportunity, but when they enter the regular freshman composition course they are often too self-conscious to participate in large class discussion. Unless a less threatening setting is provided, they may miss the opportunity for communication with their peers who are native to the language.

One example of a group activity is the discussion of an essay that has been assigned to the entire class. Questions provided by the instructor can be used to stimulate discussion if necessary. The essays chosen must be universal in some sense, not culture-bound. I have had great success, for example, with *The Diary of Anne Frank*. One person is appointed by the group to summarize the discussion. At the following meeting the summary is presented to the group for amendments and revision. The approved copy is then reproduced and distributed with the other group summaries to the class for a class discussion. Each time the group meets another member is appointed "writer"; thus the non-native student's work is presented to the entire class with the safety net of the group revision.

Another group activity is the communal creation of an outline for an essay. Again, a topic is chosen for its universality. The class has read several essays on the subject. One topic that has worked is "forms and disguises of prejudice." The group brainstorms, then puts the ideas into categories. Finally they write the outline, only a two-level outline in sentences, so that ideas of equal importance are expressed in a parallel style. In this activity the writer is more of a recorder as the whole group takes part in the writing. Non-native students often volunteer to be group writer for the outline activity.

Before any writing strategy is attempted by the groups, the strategy is discussed and illustrated. The class as a whole practices the strategy and these group activities have many benefits for non-native students. Problems with inflection and syntax disappear more quickly from both spoken and written English. However, the greatest benefit is psychological, the result of interaction with native students who are co-creators and incidentally instructors.

Forty, Foreign—and a Freshman

Ellen L. Tripp
Forsyth Technical Institute, Winston-Salem

George is fortyish, maybe thirty-fiveish: Gray hair and a care-lined face do not necessarily betoken middle age. He holds multiple degrees—at least one in business and another in law. Unfortunately they were attained in his native land, Poland, and do not automatically earn him course credits here. And so, if he decides to add an A.A.S. to his advanced degrees he will have to take college entrance exams, proficiencies, and the like. Right now he is a special credit student, taking what he elects—and what he elects, basically, is English.

I had met George, briefly, during the summer of 1981 when I was observing the ESL class in which he was an advanced student. Then in winter quarter, 1981–1982, he appeared in one of my English 101 classes, having in the interim passed his high school equivalency in English. His ESL teacher, and my own fleeting first observations, signaled me that George's major problem was (and is) lack of confidence.

And this, I am convinced, is the major problem for many of our college students who are not native speakers of English. Thus, I spent most of the 101 quarter reassuring George that he is a lot more competent in English than he thinks, and that his usual C grades were as good as—and, in fact, better than—those of most of his American-born fellows. These grades were fairly earned, not kindly given. The only general concessions I made in grading were in spelling and syntax: "errors" in both typically reflected Germanic (and, I would guess, Balto-Slavic) conventions; we cannot penalize a person for "doing what comes naturally" when what comes naturally is a learned, linguistically accepted convention in the native language.

But George did (and still does) need something more than reassurance. He, and students like him, need extra help—help we cannot give in the classroom. We can't, for instance, stop our planned program to try to explain the almost unexplainable usage of the definite and indefinite articles in English; our other students, although they don't know why, usually do the "right" thing with articles.

For George, I took my cue from our peer tutoring program (a student-to-student, subject-by-subject service of the school). But I did not want to turn George over to a tutor perhaps unknown to me and probably out of daily contact with me. Nor did I want to turn this mature professional man over to an eighteen- or twenty-year-old who had perhaps never been farther from Winston-Salem, North Carolina, than Myrtle Beach, South Carolina. Such a mismatching of ages and experiences could do more damage to a fragile self-confidence than competency-pairing could do good in the area of mechanics.

I was lucky. In that 101 section was a student of an age and experience comparable to George's: Bob is retired army, served in Europe, and is settled, mature, and capable. He also happens to write exceptionally well (although his punctuation is not always as textbook-accurate as that of George who has just learned it). But even if Bob did not write as coherently and clearly as he does, I would have solicited him for George's tutor: The age and experience compatibility counted more than did A-competency (Bob's term grade was, as a matter of fact, a B). Obviously we cannot use as tutors students who are mediocre (at best) in the subject but neither do we have to search for the "best" student to help our new-to-English student. We *do* have to attempt to match backgrounds and interests as best we can.

Having paired George and Bob in this particular situation, I was not called upon for a great deal of extra aid. I had George show Bob all of his graded exercises, tests, and papers so they could work on specific problems. At times I called their attention to continuing problems, such as article usage. I was always available after class to talk to George, to reassure him.

Did George progress during this quarter? Yes! Will he continue to make comparable progress? I don't know. As this is being written, he is in my 102 class but we are just settling down to composing, after several weeks of preparing for the research paper, and I have not yet paired him with another student. He will, I am sure, progress—because of his motivation if not because of my efforts (and this is true of every student that I have taught in similar circumstances)—but there may well be a leveling off in the rate of progress.

I do like to think, however, that the tutoring which I instigated and the support that I have given, and continue to give, make the progress smoother and more rapid. I do know that George, like others in similar circumstances, does not want favors or inflated grades. He wants to learn English and, at this stage, the place to learn it is in the regular classroom, as a regular student with no more extra consideration than is due any student with any course-related problem.

Tutoring the Non-native Student in the Regular School Program

Elizabeth Simpson
W. F. High School, Chehalis, Washington

One of the most disconcerting problems to face in the English classroom is the student who lacks ability to speak English. In so-called hands-on courses such as music, art, and vocational or technical classes, the student can be kept interested and productive while learning English and becoming acculturated. In an English class, however, the teacher has to help the student learn rudimentary skills while teaching twenty-two other students Shakespeare or college writing. This is particularly a problem in small schools, where special classes cannot be provided and the students must be fit into the schedule wherever space is available.

Cultural differences become paramount in the English classroom. Two years ago four Laotian students walked into the first session of my sophomore literature class, armed only with smiles and a despairing note from the counselor: "Only Laong speaks English. Don't let them sit together and speak Laotian; they need to practice English. Sorry—no place else to put them." I had no warning, no materials, and no experience with non-native students. I struggled through two days and then went to the assistant superintendent, whose church had been instrumental in bringing these students to America. He told me that cultural differences would make my task even more difficult. According to him, the Laotian students would consider it insulting to be taught with primary materials. They would consider it insulting to be taught by another Laotian, particularly one their own age. And politeness demanded that they nod agreement with everything the teacher said, whether or not they understood. I was enlightened, but the problem remained. I did not solve it: A private teacher was found for the students and they were removed from my class.

This year two Cambodian students were placed in my remedial writing class. Keoung spoke a little English, Paoung almost none.

As it happened, I was developing a tutoring program for students with severe problems in English, and that provided my solution. I matched Keoung and Paoung with a volunteer tutor from our honors English program. Geoff met with them for an hour each morning, and they attended my writing class for an hour each afternoon. I initially asked Geoff to cover general rules with them. His first job was to teach them to identify nouns and verbs and learn verb forms. As the term progressed, I gave Geoff the work they were having trouble with in the writing class, and he went over it with them, giving them other examples to follow or samples to copy. He taught them rules to memorize and catch phrases to help them remember. In class, they would be the first to call out, "*I* before *E* except after *C*!"

The program worked well for all concerned. Geoff learned a great deal about hitherto unfamiliar culture, and his own English skills were sharpened. I benefited, for the pressure was off me and I could spend equal time with the other students in my writing class, not having to hover over the non-native students. Paoung and Keoung benefited most of all. Geoff became their friend, their link to a sometimes frighteningly different culture. When they told him they understood something, he could stay after them until he was assured they were not being merely polite. They could ask him questions they were shy about asking in class. And most important, Paoung developed English skills to a survival level and Keoung became fluent in writing, speaking, and understanding.

The idea worked, of course, because of a humane, patient, caring young man and a flexible school schedule. It worked because of three people sitting down together, one sharing his skills and knowledge with the others. That, of course, is the essence not only of teaching, but of the cross-cultural understanding which is vital to us if we are to make our newest students feel at home.

Using Peer Groups in the Composition Classroom

Nina D. Ziv
Seton Hall University

Most colleges and universities in the United States require non-native students to take the TOEFL (Test of English as a Foreign Language) as part of the admission process. While this examination is a good measure of a student's reading comprehension, it does not indicate if a student is a competent writer; in fact, many students who are admitted to regular liberal arts programs on the basis of their test scores have difficulty in their freshman composition courses. Teachers who have these students find that there is not enough time in class to devote to their specific writing problems and will frequently confer with them outside of class on a regular basis. Though conferences are beneficial, these students often need additional help. One source of help which is readily available and often overlooked by the teacher is that of the student's peers.

One of the best ways of utilizing the help of peers is to set up peer response groups. The purpose of these groups is to give students the opportunity to get responses to their writing from someone other than the teacher. In my class, the peer response session is the first stage of the draft process my students use when they write their papers. Thus, the students bring in their initial drafts and read them to a group of four or five of their peers. Each peer then comments orally and in writing on the writer's work. After this session, the students use the peer group comments to write another draft. To make sure that the responses are useful to the writer, I train students to use a hierarchy of responses when they react to their fellow students' papers. Thus I suggest that their initial responses be directed toward the writer's ideas, and that only after this initial reaction should they attend to the lexical and syntactical problems in the text. At this stage, they may also point out errors in punctuation, spelling, and grammar to the writer.

51

For foreign students, the peer response sessions can be very beneficial: For example, one of the major problems these students have is tailoring their writing to native American audiences. Thus a student in my class who recently emigrated from Italy wrote a paper about the internal politics of his country and mentioned various political parties without indicating which part of the political spectrum they represented. When the student read his paper to his peers, they responded with bewilderment because they lacked the necessary background to understand the writer's arguments. Indeed, the peers told the student that while they were interested in reading about Italian politics, they needed a more detailed explanation of the political parties he had discussed.

Peers can also help non-native writers of English with their grammar, spelling, and punctuation errors. Often it is simply a matter of alerting them about the mistakes they are making. A case in point was a student who consistently made subject-verb agreement errors in her papers. Though I had pointed out such errors during my conferences with this student, I could not give her the constant help that she needed. I decided to alert her peers to the problem, and the next time the peer groups met, this student's group spent almost the entire session explaining her errors to her and helping her to correct them. The peers in that particular group continued to help the non-native student with her problem, and by the end of the semester she had no subject-verb agreement errors in her papers. While it is impossible to attribute this achievement to her peers alone, it is clear that they played a significant part in her progress.

Peer groups are not the panacea for the writing problems of non-native writers of English. However, if a teacher and the native American peers in the classroom work together, they can create an environment in which such students will have an excellent chance to develop their writing abilities.

Peer Teaching
Using Children's Stories

Walter McClennen
Framingham Public Schools, Massachusetts

One of the most effective techniques used by English as a Second Language (ESL) teachers can be quite easily adapted to a middle or high school peer teaching situation. The teacher will only need access to some good children's storybooks and thirty to sixty minutes to train the student tutors. After the initial training, the teacher will have to check up on the tutor and limited speaker of English to ensure proper practices and to observe student progress. As a result of the use of this technique, not only will the ESL student progress in English, but the English-speaking peer tutor will gain in writing skills and summarizing and spelling abilities besides learning what it feels like to teach and be a responsible, helpful member of society.

Briefly stated, the technique is to use, via a simple but very structured process, highly pictorial, colorful, and enjoyable children's books to teach both vocabulary and syntax as well as to develop oral and reading and writing skills in English.

Book Selection

The selection of an effective book is the first and undoubtedly the most important step in the process, and because of its importance, it should remain the prerogative of the teacher. There are three things to consider to ensure that a good book is chosen.

1. The story must have a fairly clear story line. It should contain either a sense of humor or adventure, or it should appeal to the listener's feelings in some other fairly obvious way. Very subtle story lines are hard for students who are limited in English to understand.

2. The pictures should be clear and preferably colorful. One illustration per page is best. Visually, the book should give an image of pictures rather than words as you look at the total effect of each page. Either hazy pictures or many illustrations per page can easily confuse non-native students as they try to understand the basic story line. If two overriding factors had to be listed as bases for successful book selection, they would be humor and color.

3. The greater the number of pictures that are large and that clearly show a variety of objects and actions, the better the chance for strong student progress in the new language.

Method—Nine Easy Steps

After the book is selected and a student has been chosen and trained to tutor the non-native (ESL) student, the process can be carried out by the tutor. It is quite structured because the goal is to obtain specific language growth in all four areas: listening, speaking, reading, and writing.

The book is *not* read to the ESL student. Before the student sees it, either the teacher or the tutor must have read it. They must decide which tense the story will be told in and what will be said with each page of the story as it is shown. Ideally, the story, as adapted, should be neatly written on a duplicator master before starting the series of lessons. The adapted story can be from a half-page (for beginner ESL students) to three pages (for advanced students) in length. It should follow the same story line as the original but should be restricted to one tense form (sometimes two) and should have a highly restricted vocabulary content. Many children's stories have very difficult vocabulary. An important step in this technique is to know your student's ESL level well enough so as to screen out the words that are far too difficult, but to leave a sufficient number of challenging words in the story.

The most effective and natural tense to use is the past simple (preterit). However, stories can be adapted to the present tense (both the simple and progressive forms) and to the past progressive tense if some ingenuity is applied.

Step 1: Tell the simplified story to the student, showing each page as the narrative progresses. Frequently it is advisable to do this several times to get the process started. Some key objects can be pointed out, but the initial goal is to have the student hear and see the basic story without extensive instruction.

Step 2: Explain the vocabulary. A list of twenty to forty key words of the story should be shown to the ESL student. Usually half of these are verbs and half are other parts of speech, predominantly nouns and adjectives. Many of these words should also appear in the adapted story on the duplicator master version. The ESL student should copy these words in a vocabulary notebook. Meaning should be conveyed either via pointing to the object or action as seen in the illustrations of the book, or by the tutor acting out the action or drawing the object (if it is not shown in the book). When the list is completed, the tutor should read the list aloud to the ESL student and then help the student read each word aloud.

Step 3: The tutor tells the story again, emphasizing the vocabulary that was recently explained.

Step 4: The ESL student then receives the adapted version of the story and follows along as the tutor reads it. (The issue of reading *per se* will not be discussed in the description of this method. This technique is not a replacement for a balanced phonics and reading program. Its goal is as much oral acquisition as it is the actual reading of the story.) Depending on the reading and ESL level of the student, and depending on the difficulty of the story adaptation, the ESL student then reads either individual words, several sentences, or the whole story with the support and encouragement of the tutor.

Step 5: Ten to twenty comprehension questions are asked by the tutor. The tutor must formulate the questions in such a way that the response is in the same tense as that in which the story was presented. The questions should not be very difficult. They should require recall of the basic facts of the story. The goal is to encourage the ESL student to use English to answer simple informational questions.

Step 6: Next these oral questions are given in writing to the student, who is then directed to read and answer the questions. The tutor helps with the process, not only in the meaning area but also in the areas of sentence formation and spelling. When completed, the ESL student will read the answers.

Step 7: The student now tells the tutor the story in his or her own words.

Step 8: The ESL student then writes his or her own version of the story. This may be three or four sentences in length or it may be a page or two. The only restriction is that it be in the same tense as that used in the tutor's original presentation.

Step 9: The tutor or teacher corrects the student's story and then the student copies it over neatly for a subsequent reading to the class. A file of these stories should be kept throughout the year.

Reinforcing Activities

There are dozens of reinforcing activities that can be used as the tutor practices this method. Listed below are a number that have proven effective, but different teachers will certainly come up with others.

1. Sentence formation: Any word that is presented to an ESL student should be used in a sentence by the tutor. Then the student should be asked to use that word in a spoken or written sentence sometime in the same or the next class.

2. Fill-ins: Use of the new vocabulary to complete sentences with missing words also serves to give the student practice in correct usage of the new word.

3. Oral questions: Any question that utilizes the new word gives the ESL student an opportunity to correctly use the word.

4. Vocabulary cue-card box: All new words learned during the year can be written on individual flash cards and stored for future quizzing of the student.

5. Taping the story: If a tape recorder is available, the ESL student will enjoy reading or telling the story onto the tape and then listening to the play-back.

6. Student questions: If two or more students are receiving tutoring help, they should be encouraged to ask each other questions about the story as the pages of the book are turned by the tutor. This gives practice in question formation. The tutor may have to "model" these questions to help in this sentence pattern. If only one student is being tutored, the tutor can ask a classmate to join in the question and answer time.

7. Spelling quiz: Clusters of ten to twenty words can be reinforced by having the student take them home and copy them

in preparation for a spelling quiz the next day. In the quiz, by using the words in sentences, the student will get further listening practice besides the spelling practice.

Training

The training required is basically a sharing with the student tutor the information presented in the previous two sections. It can be done quite simply by supplying a list of the nine steps to the student tutor and explaining why each step is important. Such a list should also include a list of reinforcing activities. The prospective tutor should understand well that learning a language involves the "Double Fours": (1) listening, speaking, reading, and writing, and (2) sound units, word meaning, sentence formation, and general meaning (including such practical considerations as idioms). Next the teacher must show the tutor an example of a storybook that will be used and show the tutor how such a story can be simplified so as to teach one tense form. Finally, the student should be given a book and told to form the vocabulary list, and to write the simplified version and the possible comprehension questions that will be needed. After the teacher has done this, the tutor will be ready either to start, or to watch the teacher do some of the first steps to get a feel for the speed and style of such work.

If a teacher has a group of students who are interested, it would be well worth it to spend one or two afternoons after school or during recess to give more extensive training, including some practice role-playing to provide some real experience before they start the actual teaching.

Some Books That Have Worked

Following is a list of storybooks that have been very successful in the teaching of ESL students by trained ESL teachers. There certainly are many others that can be found in the local library. If the process is followed as described, these and other books should be successful in helping students who are limited in the use of English to learn the new language via tutoring from their classmates.

Aliki. *Go Tell Aunt Rhody.* New York: Macmillan, 1974.

Aliki. *The Story of Johnny Appleseed.* Englewood Cliffs, N. J.: Prentice-Hall, 1963.

Bruna, Dick. *The Sailor.* New York: Methuen, 1979.

Burton, Virginia Lee. *The Little House.* Boston: Houghton-Mifflin, 1941.

Carlson, Bernice, and Ristina Wigg. *We Want Sunshine in Our House.* Nashville, Tenn.: Abingdon, 1973.

Ipcar, Dahlov. *The Land of Flowers.* New York: The Viking Press, 1974.

Keats, Ezra Jack. *John Henry.* New York: Pantheon, 1965.

Leaf, Munro. *The Story of Ferdinand.* New York: The Viking Press, 1938.

Lobel, Anita. *The Troll Music.* New York: Harper & Row, 1966.

McClosky, Robert. *Burt Dow—Deep-Water Man.* New York: The Viking Press, 1963.

Pendery, Rosemary. *A Home for Hopper.* New York: William Morrow, 1971.

Polito, Leo. *Emmet.* New York: Charles Scribner's Sons, 1971.

Rey, H. A. *Curious George.* Boston: Houghton-Mifflin, 1941.

Ungerer, Tomi. *The Beast of Monsieur Racine.* New York: Farrar, Straus and Giroux, 1971.

Ungerer, Tomi. *Crictor.* New York: Harper & Row, 1969.

Ungerer, Tomi. *Emile.* New York: Harper & Row, 1960.

Ward, Lynd. *The Silver Pony.* Boston: Houghton-Mifflin, 1973.

A New Dimension for the Non-native Student

Sonja Lutz
Belle Glade, Florida

Four teenagers nervously shuffled their feet and stared at the ceiling while practicing their dialogue.

"Où est la bibliothèque, Salusa?"

"Allez tout droite et tournez à gauche."

"Where is the library, Salusa?"

"Go straight ahead and turn to the left."

The class appeared to be a typical French class practicing their dialogues, but if visitors were to listen carefully, they would find this wasn't so.

In reality, the group was composed of six Haitian students who were desperately trying to adjust to a new culture and language, and six French II students who were trying to understand another culture and improve their French.

I never knew whether the class was formed by coincidence or design, but after two weeks of not knowing what to do with either group, a plan took shape. My goal was to give each set of students some amount of proficiency in the other's language.

The first thing I did was to pack all the audio-lingual books and tapes into the closet. I ordered a French grammar workbook to provide some structure to the students' needs.

While the workbooks were on their way, I divided the students into three groups of four, each with two Haitian and two French II students. It was after the formation of these groups that real peer teaching began.

We went on mini-field trips which the class affectionately dubbed "The Big Vocabulary Hunt." We took walks to grocery and department stores where we explored vocabulary. As the students saw items of interest, they laboriously copied their newly found words in their notebooks while repeating them after me. Back in class, the students wrote dialogues, first in French and then in

English, using their newly found words. The dialogues were practiced and acted out in both languages. Whenever anyone got stuck there was always someone in the group to help.

Experiences were provided for any need that might occur. When one student said he was having trouble with directions, a whole week's work started. The students went on walks, with the leader giving directions in his or her language, only to reverse leaders and languages on the return trip.

Scavenger hunts were devised with complicated directions being written out in one language or the other. During this activity, students were deliberately made dependent on one another. As a follow-up, students worked independently on worksheets which reviewed the directions they had followed during the scavenger hunt.

Underlying the study of French and English, constant cultural sharing began to emerge. At Christmas, the group went caroling in both languages and provided a community club with a program. Trips were taken to a French and an American restaurant. The class created original puppet shows in both languages and gave them at the elementary schools. Who better could have won the Brotherhood Week bulletin board competition than this class?

Aside from the language and cultural activities, there was also a sharing of problems. The French II students became increasingly aware of the loneliness and rejection the Haitian students were experiencing. Salusa was particularly concerned about being called a refugee. "Only in this country am I a refugee," he said. "I am a Haitian everywhere. I know what I am." Although this student was subjected to the taunts of other students in the lunchroom, he felt the sympathetic support of the members of the French class. He was able to follow the good advice of his classmates and ignore his tormentors. After several weeks, no more was heard of the problem.

At the end of the year the Haitian students were learning English rapidly, and although the French students had covered less material than normal, they were using the French they had learned. Maxin, who in the beginning of the year was suspended because the only words he spoke in English were curse words, is now quieter and is often praised by the other students. Salusa has so successfully mastered English that he is succeeding well in his social studies and science classes. He is now reading on the tenth grade level, which I can't say about many of my English-speaking students.

There is also evidence that the other half of the class benefited from the experience. One of the French II students, a clerk at the pharmacy after school, is able to handle simple problems in French. The French students are not afraid of the language. Their experience with the Haitian students made the speaking of a foreign language real.

To be sure, there are purists of French inflection who would despair because my students speak a substandard French. However, I feel that this class accomplished as much as or more than the ordinary language class. Who is really to say that one native speaker is superior to another? How many students will have had such first-hand insights into another culture? It is certain my students will remember more than the isolated vocabulary words that happen to take their fancy, or the dialogues that have been so faithfully memorized.

Southern Florida may be one of the few areas that can capitalize on Haitian students, but there are possibilities in other schools. I can visualize Spanish students being paired with English students on both the elementary and secondary levels. We can take advantage of the non-native English speaker and provide language learning as well as cultural enrichment for our potential language students.

How much richer will be the experience of the language student who has daily encounters with native speakers of that language. At the same time, how much more quickly the bilingual student will be assimilated into the mainstream of school society by such an experience.

Kids Can Be ESL Teachers

Helen S. Wagner
Hannah Middle School, East Lansing, Michigan

When in doubt, ask the kids! That's good advice for experienced and beginning teachers alike. When a problem arises in the classroom, thirty students can generate far more ideas than one teacher —and a surprising percentage of the ideas are usable.

Many times I have used this technique with students, but one time in particular stands out in my mind. Budget cuts precluded the addition of specialized personnel to assist classroom teachers, and non-native students were assigned to regular classrooms. As an English teacher, I felt well qualified to teach all phases of my subject, but I had no training whatsoever in teaching non-English-speaking students. Yet, on the first day of school, there in my heterogeneous seventh grade class sat Adnan from Turkey and Kato from Japan, both smiling shyly and not understanding a word spoken by any of us.

It soon became apparent that I had neither the time nor the skills to help these boys—so I turned to the kids. "What can we do to help these boys learn our language?" I asked. The response was instantaneous and included such top-of-the-head ideas as (1) get the librarian to read to them, (2) get a parent-volunteer to tutor them, (3) "you" could give *us* worksheets to do while you teach *them*. The assigned work for that night was: "Think through the problem and see what ideas materialize."

The following day a variety of ideas was submitted but still confusion reigned. Finally someone said, "Let's teach them ourselves," and the plan was underway. Students prepared lists of words they considered important. The same words appeared on many lists and others were inappropriate (*kangaroo, koala, lizard* —in a Michigan classroom?). About this time leaders began to evolve from the group. Discussions (and debates) resounded through the room, a few desks were pounded, a few tears were shed. Finally, it was agreed that the idea of word lists alone wouldn't work. All agreed to think about the problem one more night.

During the next class period a plan began to take shape: Each student would be responsible for planning and tutoring one class period. A committee of three, later known as The Wheels (to keep things rolling) formulated the procedure. Rules were established:

Each student (some later chose to work in pairs) will:

1. tutor one hour and return to class five minutes before the hour ends
2. decide on the content for the hour
3. write detailed plans and lists of words to be "taught"
4. submit plans to The Wheels one week before the assigned tutoring-time
5. explain or revise plans as required by The Wheels
6. provide Adnan and Kato with review sheets and supply a duplicate sheet to the room librarian for the master copy
7. prepare any aids needed
8. make arrangements for use of school materials or locations
9. spend the first ten minutes of the hour reviewing the previous day's lesson with the foreign students
10. check on and make up own assignment for the period absent from class

Following explanations and discussions, the group approved the rules by a unanimous vote and work began.

The Wheels were swamped with plans which came rolling in. Some of the first plans were approved with few corrections but many others needed revision. In fact, The Wheels were so busy with this task that they found it necessary to delegate other responsibilities: Two students were assigned to confer with individual tutors and prepare a clear and colorful schedule board; a group of three was dispatched to the principal's office to obtain approval for our project; one girl designed and made name-tag passes since students would be moving about the building at various times; one pair checked out taping equipment from the media center; another group obtained art supplies for the room—and so it went.

Finally, the big day arrived. It was time for the first lesson. Phillip was in charge. As our star athlete, he chose, not surprisingly, to "teach" about sports equipment and games. The coach had agreed to let him use the equipment room. Not only did Adnan and Kato learn the words *bat, baseball, basketball, glove, soccer,* and so on, but they also learned by doing: shooting baskets, pitching, kicking, passing, and the like. I was not surprised when they returned to class on time, with eyes sparkling.

The next day Tammy picked up the review sheet and left with her charges for the cafeteria. To her, nothing was more essential than food. The cafeteria workers put Tammy's handprinted labels beside the baked chicken, potatoes, green beans, milk, and cookies. Tasting, smelling, and looking made this one of the favorite lessons. *Knife, fork, tray, glass,* as well as *please* and *thank you,* formed this lesson.

Additional sessions focused on various kinds of words and related statements/questions. The following samples show the variety of lessons:

1. Items in a classroom: *pencil, paper, globe, map.*
2. Locations: *auditorium, rest rooms, wood shop, library.*
3. Outdoors: *grass, shrubs, trees, fence.*
4. Foods: (Bill brought fruit, carrots, candy, gum, cookies.)
5. Musical instruments: (Instruments and players were borrowed from the band room through courtesy of band director.)
6. Money: (Jeff used real money plus Monopoly money.)
7. Articles of clothing: (Jane made paper dolls and also used her little sister's Ken and Barbie dolls.)
8. Buildings: *the Capitol, filling stations, churches, houses.* (Tom and Aaron combined slides with mounted magazine pictures.)
9. Sounds: (Nancy made a cassette of familiar noises: door bell, horn, breaking glass, squealing brakes.)
10. The alphabet: (Ellen and Alex taught how to print, write, and say the letters.)
11. Our government system: (Chris used encyclopedia charts and later his father took the foreign students and Chris to the Capitol.)

Enthusiasm reigned supreme for several weeks. In fact, high interest was maintained until the winter holidays. Since all students were aware of the information being taught, constant review occurred—on the playground, in the lunch line, in the halls. I felt like the sorcerer's apprentice. One thing led to another and there seemed no way to stop "the program." But—it finally stopped itself. *The boys learned to speak English.*

The final first semester project assignment for the class was an oral report based on research on any subject of interest to the student. Adnan and Kato were expected to participate too. Their assignment: Make an oral report to your class about your own country. In halting English (and some strange sentence structures), but with much pride, both boys delivered their oral reports. The applause and standing ovations were sincerely given and truly deserved.

The following day The Wheels asked for five minutes of class time. Members of the class had contributed money to purchase real dictionaries, which were happily presented to Adnan and Kato. And, it was agreed that the tutoring program had served its purpose and was no longer needed.

Any educational project must be followed by an evaluation and this was no exception. Was the project valuable? Was it a waste of time? Was anything learned by the "regular" students? Were the objectives met? Formally, I really can't say, but during this time:

1. I never saw a misspelled word on a list, poster, or any teaching materials (although I continued to see some on regular assignments).
2. I frequently heard arguments about standard English versus slang and dialect. "Why can't I teach them 'He be the principal'?"
3. I saw reference books constantly being researched for pictures and accurate information to "teach."
4. I observed students cooperating in small and large groups as they discussed, justified, compromised, and made decisions.
5. I helped individual students organize their time, write coherently, and venture into the realm of effective communication.
6. I saw evidence of real concern and caring for fellow human beings by bullies, loners, social butterflies, and many others.
7. I heard students contacting, interviewing, and explaining plans to adults.
8. I watched novices edit, revise, and rewrite information.
9. I thumbed through a master notebook and file of materials prepared and compiled by students.
10. I watched "klutzes" using delicate materials to prepare visual and sound materials to supplement their plans.
11. And—I helped address newsletters written by students to explain their project to parents.

Was it educationally of value? *Absolutely!* I learned too much— about kids. And with today's decreasing budgets, more teachers may find these suggestions helpful for their non-native students. Our project was effective because we dared to try a different approach. Students assumed an unusual degree of responsibility and served as ESL teachers. A teacher should never underestimate kids. And the next time you're stuck with a problem, just ask *them*, the kids, for solutions.

3 Reading and Writing Instruction

Visual Imagery Instruction to Improve Reading Comprehension

Samuel A. Perez
University of Texas at Arlington

Linguistically different pupils who are having trouble compre-hending what they read often lack the ability to form visual images from reading material. The linguistically different pupil may actually "read" a selection reasonably well, decoding each word accurately and perhaps even reading with proper expression. But, when asked "What mental pictures did the reading passage suggest to you?" the answer you get may be, "I don't know."

The visual images we hope our pupils will form when reading are created in the mind of the reader by the descriptions or ideas found in the reading material. The process of translating these words into images is made possible by two things working together —the reader's imagination and understanding of the reading material. Developing visual imagery grows out of practice in trying to visualize the story settings, characters, objects, and story action of reading material. Although pupils differ greatly in their ability to visualize what is read, those who have this skill tend to have better comprehension and retention of what they read.

The suggestions for teaching visual imagery described in this article can be used to increase the visual imagery of linguistically different pupils. As pupils become more skilled in visualizing what they read, the ability to comprehend and retain what is read will also improve. An additional benefit of visual imagery instruction is that it will promote the development of imagination, listening skills, and oral language ability in linguistically different pupils. The suggested activities for increasing visual imagery can be used with groups of pupils or individual pupils at any age or grade level.

The initial step in introducing visual imagery to linguistically different pupils is to have pupils visualize a few specific things: a favorite person or place, a prized personal possession, or a special event or happening. For example, ask pupils to visualize their own bedroom, and answer specific questions about their image. These questions might include: "Where is your bed located in the room?" "What colors do you see in the room?" "What objects in the room are most vivid to you?" Another example of an introductory visualizing exercise is to have pupils think of a relative or close friend whom they have not seen in some time. Ask them to try to visualize the facial features of the person, their body posture, or the clothes they are wearing.

Other visual imagery activities include having linguistically different pupils visualize the color of an approaching car which gradually changes color as they are visualizing it, and encouraging pupils to visualize themselves walking on the ceiling or flying over tree tops. An important procedure in using these introductory activities is to arrange pupils into pairs or small groups to share their mental pictures with others, and to listen to the visual images of their fellow pupils.

After introducing visual imagery to linguistically different pupils in the preceding activities, have pupils form mental pictures related to story selections that you read aloud to them. Be sure to choose stories or passages that are full of visual descriptions. Before you start reading a selection, ask pupils to try to form specific visual images as they listen to the words. As you read the selection aloud to pupils, occasionally have them close their eyes and picture what you are reading. Once in a while you may want to pause to discuss with pupils their mental pictures or to write a descriptive word or phrase from the selection on the chalkboard. You may also occasionally pause to pose questions, but not necessarily to seek answers. For example, after reading "The car moved slowly through the city streets," stop to ask "What model and color is the car?" "What buildings do you see in the city?" "What other cars do you see on the street?"

The next stage in developing the visual imagery of linguistically different pupils is to have them describe the mental pictures they see after they have read a passage. Be sure to have them read material that is concrete or highly stimulating to imagination. Pupils should also be cautioned to first form visual images after reading the passage before they try to visualize while reading. After pupils have read a story selection, first ask them to describe their visual images associated with the passage. It may help to ask them to tell what personal experiences the passage reminded them of. Then encourage pupils to supply details not included in the reading selection. This can be done by asking specific questions about details. You should accept all reasonable answers and praise pupils for their detailed images.

A follow-up activity after linguistically different pupils have developed skill in forming mental pictures of what they read is to have pupils draw or illustrate the mental images related to reading material. Although not all reading material can be easily illustrated, certain objects, persons, and scenes can be drawn by linguistically different pupils. Their drawings do not have to be great art or very elaborate. You should accept whatever the pupils produce. Since many linguistically different pupils would probably rather draw than read, do not let them spend too much time on their illustrations. And be sure to provide opportunities for linguistically different pupils to explain or tell about their illustrations to other pupils, either in pairs or small groups. Other follow-up visual imagery activities include having pupils pantomime the mental pictures formed from reading, having them suggest how stories could be made into television dramas with their favorite TV actors and actresses, and having them write descriptions of the visual images associated with what they are reading.

The suggestions for increasing visual imagery described in this article can be particularly valuable in teaching linguistically different pupils for two important reasons. First, an increase in the linguistically different pupil's ability to form visual images will lead to better comprehension of what is read. Second, the opportunity to talk about, answer questions about, or write about their mental images will give linguistically different pupils much needed practice in using language in formulating and expressing complex thoughts. The results will be a significant contribution to the linguistically different pupil's development in all the English language arts.

Teaching Latin to the Remedial

Rebecca Hodgkinson
Duncan-Russell High School, Tracy, California

"I can't read good now. How's Latin gonna help that?" was the initial response when I introduced vocabulary through roots, prefixes, and suffixes in my remedial reading classes. One year later, this same student clamors for attention to be the one to define *C'est la Vie! Viva la Raza!* and *convivial* using his newfound key to the English language—root words.

Spanish, Portuguese, and Anglo students compete to unlock the meaning of new words through a basic understanding of how words are formed. In my continuation high school language arts classroom, I use a multilingual vocabulary approach in attempts to reach and relate language to the diverse cultures represented.

Teaching vocabulary through sight identification of roots can be accomplished in a variety of ways. The torture time of memorizing lists of words, never employed in daily use by a student and seemingly irrelevant to our age, no longer exists for my students.

The roots and words formed by these roots are introduced on a weekly basis. The following would by a typical weekly exercise.

ante (before)	*anti* (against)	*circum* (around)
contra (against)	*de* (down)	*fore* (before)
inter (between)	*intra* (within)	*non* (not)

antebellum, noncombatant, intrastate, forefather, antislavery, contraband, contrabando (Spanish), *interval, dethrone, detroner* (French), *circumnavigate, none, nul* (French), *forethought, demote, circumference, circunferencio* (Spanish), *antinuclear, intraregional, contraband, intermission, intermittent* (French), *circumvent, interchange, intercambio* (Spanish), *forewarn, international, internacional* (Spanish), *antedated, foresee, intercultural, intramuscular, intravenous, intraveineux* (French), *nonfiction, nonsense.*

Using the above information, the student's first assignment would be to simply list the words under the common root. Then the class would define the words through the root's meaning. Students usually enjoy this exercise since it relies on both creative and logical thinking. Many times, words contain more than one root, prefix, or suffix; hence the student inadvertently receives more information or reinforcement of past learning. For instance, *ante* (before) with *antebellum* (before war), as *bell* means *war* (*rebellion, bellicose,* and so on).

Other variations of this instructive technique can enhance the lessons. (1) Students can draw language trees for roots, showing how they are evidenced in a variety of languages. (2) Students can investigate word origins; therefore, dictionary work becomes part of the experience.

Once the students have learned a bank of roots, prefixes, and suffixes, two more lively learning techniques can be introduced:

> *Vocabulary Bingo.* This game is the fastest and most enjoyable method of reinforcing vocabulary. Students are given a blank bingo card, basically a card with twenty-five empty squares. From a list of forty roots the students make their own cards, entering the root only. The teacher then gives the root definition. The student must know that *aqua* on the card means *water* in order to place a chip on the correct square. After I taught roots for two months, my students were able to learn them permanently in one hour by quick association, which enabled them to win more games.

> *Creation of New Words.* The students make up new words using the roots, prefixes, and suffixes that they have learned. For example, *aquahomo* (*waterman*) or *legacide* (*law killer,* or *rule breaker*). Once the students have developed a bank of roots to work from, they enjoy making their own words.

In short, teaching vocabulary through roots, prefixes, and suffixes gives the students from various cultural groups a better understanding of both English and their native language.

Pablo and *el diccionario*

Doris Spraberry
Abilene High School, Texas

Pablo was failing Sophomore English. The grade book remained pristine beside his name. A deep sadness filled me as I stared at it for a moment and then shifted my gaze to the small, dark teenager who was Pablo. He glanced up briefly and I used that opportunity to call him to my desk.

"Pablo," I began quietly, "I am very concerned. You have not turned in a single paper this entire six weeks. You know what that means."

He did not answer.

"Pablo, I want to help you, but I don't know what you need from me unless you tell me. Why have you not done the work?"

His eyes were shuttered as he shifted uncomfortably in the conference chair I kept beside me. "Please, Pablo, won't you let me help you?"

"Joo can't help me. I gonna quit soon."

"But why? You have come so far, and I know that you are an intelligent young man."

He squared his shoulders slightly at the word *man*.

"Aww, the teacher they all just pass me along."

This time he looked up. There was fire in his eyes.

"Very well, Pablo. Maybe you are right. But since you are going to quit anyway, won't you just tell me what you see as the problem?"

There was a moment when I thought he was about to get up from the chair and go back to his assigned seat, but the moment passed.

"It is the reading—the stories," he said.

"You don't like them?" We were in literature. I considered it to be my specialty.

"Naw, not that. I like them some. It is the reading. You know—the words."

"Why, you have read aloud and you read very well."

74

"Sure I can. I ain't no dummy. I can read the words, but they don' say to me what they say to maybe you."

I knew exactly what he meant. Pablo was a word caller. He could call almost any word because he was intelligent enough to catch on to our system, but that did not mean that he knew what he was saying.

Suddenly an idea was born. If we had been in a comic strip, a light bulb would have flashed over my head.

"Pablo, you can't quit school yet because you aren't old enough. You have to stay. Would you be willing to do something for me?"

"I guess maybe."

"Would you go through that story we had today and find, say, ten words that gave you trouble and then get their Spanish equivalent for me? Just write it all out."

"Joo mean do that question sheet *and* them words?"

"No, no. Forget the question sheet. Just get the words. Maybe you can put it all down for someone else who may have trouble with them after you are gone."

"Joo mean some other Tex-Mex?" He was smiling.

"Something like that. What I have in mind is keeping your list for future reference. That way when I have another student who comes from a home in which Spanish is spoken, I can pull out your list and use it to help him—that is, if you don't mind."

"Naww, I don' mind."

He got up and went back to his desk. A moment later he was hard at work. Once he got up and crossed to the reference books we kept on a shelf in the corner, to pick up a Spanish-English dictionary. When the bell rang, he stopped by my desk. "I think maybe I take this book, this dictionary, home with me. O.K.?"

"Sure," I replied trying to hold in my delight. That book had remained unopened on the shelf ever since I bought it the previous year.

The next day Pablo handed me a list of twenty-five words, all neatly written out with Spanish equivalents beside them. "Maybe I do them questions you had yesterday if you take them late," he said.

"Oh, I think that is the least I can do after you did all this for me," I replied.

Our deal was struck. After that, Pablo turned in all of his work, some of it complete and some of it not, but nevertheless it was attempted. Every story we read elicited a list of words in Spanish and in English. I was elated with the progress that he made. He seemed to have a far better grasp of the meaning of the stories now that he had come to use this method of finding out what an English word meant in Spanish. He was even more interested in its English definition.

His answers were not always the best, perhaps, but they were answers, and they demonstrated thought. What more could I want? An example of his handling of the literature-related questions is best demonstrated by the following answer he gave once, when I had asked for a character sketch:

> The English word "sketch" is "boceto" in Spanish. It means "outline." I think you want me to outline this man's character. I am no drawer. I think you want this outline in words. But not in one words or two words like you teach outlining. So I say he is "simpatico." That is Spanish. It mean he is nice guy. I find no good words for simpatico in the dictionary. It is a good Spanish word. I say he is simpatico because he help that guy when he need somebody.

Carefully, I wrote in the margin, "Thanks for this word. Your explanation is 'simpatico.' Did I use the word correctly?"

We finished out the year, Pablo and I. He passed Sophomore English. The times were few and far between that he failed to turn in a paper after he began to think about Spanish equivalents and to recognize that I welcomed their inclusion and explanations in his work. Sometimes the only thing he turned in was the Spanish-English word list, but I gave him credit; both he and I knew Pablo had found a way to cope. Best of all, I too had found a way.

A Functional Approach to Vocabulary Instruction

Stanley J. Zehm
Washington State University, Pullman

One of the first tasks facing regular classroom teachers in the elementary school who are assigned the additional responsibility of developing the expressive fluency of non-native speakers of English is to assist these students in acquiring a functional vocabulary. With the tools of a functional vocabulary, limited English-speaking students will be able to begin functioning in the regular classroom with increasing competence and confidence. Without these tools, such students will flounder, waste inordinate amounts of time, and cause increasing frustration to themselves and their teachers.

The strategy I will describe is a three-phased program designed to promote the rapid acquisition of a functional vocabulary by non-English-speaking children in regular classrooms. This approach is currently being utilized by elementary teachers in the American International School in Bangkok, Thailand.

Phase One—Vocabulary Building

This effective strategy begins with activities designed to get a selected list of high frequency words into the receptive and expressive vocabularies of the target group. These words are chosen by the individual teachers from such sources as the "Dolch List," the basal reader, and the teacher's observations of individual students' needs. The activities have a multisensory design and are carefully constructed to appeal to as many senses as possible. The instructional goal of these activities is to get the new vocabulary into student's eyes, ears, mouths, hands, and whole bodies as quickly as possible.

One typical activity requires students to identify words written on flash cards prepared by their teachers. On the reverse side of

77

these laminated flash cards, the teachers have glued pictures that appropriately identify each word. The student who cannot identify the printed word may turn the card over for the pictorial clue.

A number of similar activities, all aimed at providing engaging presentation, practice, and review have been prepared to foster rapid vocabulary recognition. The key to the success of these activities resides in three prerequisites: (1) the functional vocabulary activities must be short, no longer than fifteen minutes; (2) they must be multisensory; and (3) they must be highly motivating (many of the activities I observed were set up on a game basis).

Phase Two—Providing Appropriate Contexts

The second phase of this vocabulary-building strategy is aimed at assisting students to utilize newly acquired vocabulary within the appropriate syntactic and semantic contexts of the English language. Consequently, most word identification activities are coupled with activities in which the words are immediately used in an oral or written context. The words *bread, milk,* and *table,* for example, could be placed in the same syntactic pattern of "This is bread," "This is milk," and "This is a table." Later these same words could be used in different syntactic and semantic contexts such as "The bread is on the table," "The milk is on the table," and "The bread and milk are on the table."

These carefully constructed activities give non-native speakers of English regular opportunities to use their newly acquired vocabulary in a context that not only promotes their communicative fluency, but also helps them begin to understand the critical importance of word order in the English language. Practice in making meaning will also help these students in decoding meaning in their reading activities.

Phase Three—Adding the Social Dimension

The third phase in developing the functional vocabularies of limited-English-speaking students extends the students' word recognition skills and their ability to use new words in appropriate syntactic and semantic contexts by adding a social dimension to language learning. Most of the activities of the first two phases described above initially require the regular classroom teacher to work with the non-English-speaking students in an individualized small-group setting. The use of teacher aides and parent volunteers can be very helpful in providing this individualized instruction. During the third phase, however, the limited-English-speaking students can gradually be grouped with regular students to promote skill in the social and pragmatic uses of English.

In this phase, teachers prepare activities of a social nature which require all students to use their functional vocabularies in order to communicate with one another. One activity that can be used to promote interstudent communication is called the "Question of the Day" activity by the elementary teachers in Bangkok's American International School. This activity begins with the teacher framing a question intended to provide a structure for student responses about things important to their immediate lives. For example, one question might be "What games do you like to play?" The teacher first addresses this question to one of the students in this mixed group of limited and proficient English-speaking students. The student responds by saying something such as "I like to play tag, jump rope, and dodgeball." The student then directs the same question, "What games do you like to play?", to the student in the next seat. Within a short period of time, all of the students in the group ask and answer the "Question of the Day." This social setting for language development provides the limited-English-speaking students with a real and comfortable context for using their newly acquired functional vocabularies. It also provides a variety of carefully controlled syntactic patterns which the students can use in communicating meaning. More important, however, it provides the limited-English-speaking students the opportunity to model the vocabulary of their English-speaking classmates within the safety of the regular elementary classroom.

Basic Vocabulary for the Limited or Non-English-speaking Student

Sylvia C. Peña
University of Houston

The three-period Montessori lesson is an effective strategy for helping limited or non-English-speaking students to function and participate in the regular classroom. Several of my student teachers have used the strategy effectively when teaching in Spanish and in teaching vocabulary in the second language. That is, the strategy can work not only in concept acquisition but in teaching basic vocabulary to speakers of English as a second language. It works best with small groups of children since it is a nonthreatening, effective way of developing vocabulary.

Basically, the strategy involves three steps: labeling, identifying, and recognizing the stimuli. The procedure is quite straightforward and is always the same so that the child can focus on what is being taught and not on the procedure itself. The teacher's instructions and expectations are also very simple and direct for the same reason. Moreoever, the child is responding to the same instructions each time a lesson is conducted and therefore need not monitor teacher-talk but rather may concentrate on the concepts. Each step is described below in more detail.

Step 1. Labeling

The teacher must use picture cards with lables such as the Developmental Learning Materials (DLM) category cards or the Dolch Popper Words. Five or six cards can be presented at a time and the teacher should select the most common words for the initial presentation; with the child sitting in front of the teacher, on the floor or at a table, one card at a time is placed, right to left, facing the child. The teacher says each word clearly as the card is placed in front of the child, and the child repeats the word. The teacher should simply say "This is _____" as the card is presented, without deviating throughout subsequent presentations. In this way, the child not only learns the pattern "This is _____" but does not have to contend with other patterns while learning the new words. If a pronunciation error is committed the teacher should go on, for the child will have several more opportunities to hear and repeat each word.

Once all the cards have been presented, the teacher should repeat the procedure two or three times, but the cards should be in a different order each time. If the lesson is conducted with several children (but no more than five or six), the teacher must listen carefully to determine that all the children are saying each word and trying to imitate correct pronunciation. More trial repetitions may be necessary when working with small groups. Once the child has seen and repeated each word and picture card with satisfactory pronunciation, the teacher goes on to the next step.

Step 2. Identifying.

This time all of the cards are placed facing the child. The teacher then says "Show me _____." The child should point to the correct item and repeat the word. Once the child has identified all of the words following the prompt "Show me _____," the teacher picks up the cards and places them in a different order. The child can be asked to close his or her eyes while the teacher does this. The teacher repeats the procedure, asking the child "Show me _____." It is important that this step be repeated at least three times to make sure that the child knows all of the words and uses satisfactory pronunciation. Again, it is not necessary to correct pronunciation errors in isolation; rather, the object is to give the child many opportunities to practice. If the child hesitates after prompting, the teacher must determine whether the child is being inattentive or having difficulty remembering the words. If it is the latter, step one may have to be repeated so the child can hear the word and repeat it before having to demonstrate the ability to associate label and picture.

Step 3. Recognizing

The third step is a test of recognition. The child must be able to point to the appropriate picture and say the word. The teacher prompts by saying "What is this?" while pointing to a card. The prompt is repeated with all the cards until the child has identified and labeled each card. The procedure is repeated and, as in steps one and two, the teacher must vary the order to make sure that the child has not simply memorized the words.

All of the above three steps constitute one lesson presentation. Once the child has successfully mastered a set of words, they become his or her words. As more lessons are presented, each time following the same three steps and using the same prompts, the child's bank of words increases. This is a concrete way for the child to realize that progress is indeed being made, and it can be further reinforced by having the child make cards of words already mastered.

The same strategy can be used to present words from the basal readers if these are being used with limited or non-English-speaking children. The teacher must ensure that if the words represent unknown concepts for the child, they must be presented with the visual representation so the child need not deal with a language and concept overload. This happens when both the language is unknown and the concept is presented in that language. By using a picture, the child has a representation of the concept to facilitate acquisition of its label in the second language.

If native English-speaking children have been presented three-step lessons and are very familiar with the procedures, they can be peer teachers and make reinforcement presentations to the limited or non-English-speaking children. The teacher must make sure that the English-speaking student has a positive attitude toward the strategy and, most important, toward the limited or non-English-speaking students. The experience must be a positive one for all involved. Moreover, to foster better relations among all of the students, the limited or non-English-speaking child can teach the English monolingual students some Spanish words, using the same three-step lessons. Both groups can gain self-esteem while learning from each other. The limited or non-English-speaking student can also learn that his or her language is valued by teacher and classmates alike, and this awareness can be the motivator for further language learning.

4 Teaching the Nonstandard Dialect Student

Teaching Sociolinguistic Differences in the Language Arts Classroom

Duane H. Roen
University of Arizona

The highly publicized Ann Arbor Decision handed down by United States District Judge Charles W. Joiner on 12 July 1979 in Detroit did much to raise public and professional awareness of the linguistic challenges facing teachers. In that case the court ruled that teachers who speak standard dialects of English must learn to recognize and accept the nonstandard dialects of their students, who in this instance were black elementary students. The court noted in this landmark decision that teachers who are unfamiliar with the linguistic features (phonological, morphological, semantic, and syntactic) of their students' nonstandard dialects may intentionally or unintentionally induce in students insecurity about the language they and their families use in the home. Such children may also feel that teachers and other speakers of standard dialects of English reject not only nonstandard dialects but also speakers of nonstandard dialects. As a result of this feeling of cultural rejection, the ability to learn to read, write, speak, or understand standard English is impaired.

In the Ann Arbor case, Judge Joiner based his decision on the expert testimony of such notable scholars as Dan Fader, William Labov, and J. L. Dillard. Their collective conviction that speakers of standard English can instill linguistic insecurity in speakers of nonstandard English is not new. Others, like James Sledd (1971) and Robbins Burling (1973) discussed the problem much earlier in this century's most socially tumultuous decade. Sledd, in particular, argued that language arts teachers who speak standard dialects are masters (the pun is intended) at promoting hypercorrection, linguistic insecurity, and even linguistic self-hatred among their students who speak nonstandard dialects of English.

The question that arises then is this: What can language arts teachers do to help their nonstandard dialect students overcome linguistic insecurity and linguistic self-hatred, especially in classrooms in which students speak a variety of social dialects? Is it possible to help speakers of dialects regarded as nonstandard feel comfortable about their linguistic identity, while at the same time encouraging speakers of dialects regarded as standard to accept dialects which they consider stigmatized?

One strategy for accomplishing both of the aforementioned goals involves some informal student research, conducted with some teacher assistance and a tape recorder. In the tradition of Labov (1964), students can elicit the speech of different speakers in different social contexts, ranging from relatively informal to relatively formal. Students then bring recordings of these speech samples to class, where they are analyzed.

There are five styles of speech that students at the secondary or collegiate levels can elicit, record, and analyze: casual speech, careful speech, reading style, word lists, and minimal pairs. Students can elicit casual speech simply by asking the informant to talk about some life-threatening experience he or she has had. In eliciting this style of speech, it is important that the informant believe that it is the dangerous experience and not his or her speech that is of interest. Like the experienced linguist, the novice fieldworker does not want to alert the informant that his or her speech is under scrutiny.

To gather careful speech, the student simply asks the informant to talk about a topic that requires less emotional involvement. Such topics include those related to career or educational goals, for example.

Reading style may be elicited by asking the informant to read a passage from a book, newspaper, or magazine. It is important that this passage include words that display some of the same linguistic idiosyncrasies that occurred in the speaker's casual and careful speech. For example, words that end in /nd/, such as *and*, as well as words that end in /iŋ/, such as *writing* and *running*, typically appear in most elicited samples of casual and careful speech. In less formal styles a word like *and* will often occur as /æn/ (*an'*) and a word like *writing* as /rayʔn/ (*writin'*). Of course, even a cursory examination of the samples of less formal speech will reveal other phonological features of interest.

To elicit a word-list speech sample, students simply compile a list of words, some of which allow the informant once again to display phonological idiosyncrasies. The list should also include some distractors to prevent the informant from knowing which phonological features are under investigation.

Asking informants to read a number of minimal pairs will elicit the most formal speech samples. A minimal pair consists of two words that have in common all but one phoneme (distinctive sound). The following are examples of minimal pairs, at least in many dialects: *bin/pin, pat/pit, brand/bland, sad/sap,* and *sanding/landing.* The list of minimal pairs, like the reading passage and word list, should include some words that allow informants to display phonological patterns appearing in less formal speech.

For the purposes of teachers in most secondary classrooms, it probably works best to have each student in the class tape a single speaker on five different occasions, each at least a day or two apart and each more formal than the preceding one. This procedure prevents the informant from guessing the precise nature of the investigator's interests.

Once all of the samples have been collected, the analysis may begin. The analysis should consist initially of counting the number of times a speaker uses a particular phonological feature in each of the five styles. The students will discover that all types of speakers will more frequently use standard forms in more formal styles. For example, students may find that *and* occurs as /æn/ rather than /ænd/ 81 percent of the time in casual speech, 73 percent of the time in careful speech, 39 percent of the time in reading, 13 percent of the time in word lists, and only 9 percent of the time in minimal pairs. These frequencies will vary from speaker to speaker, of course, especially across social classes, and lower-middle-class speakers will demonstrate the most dramatic shifts toward the standard in more formal styles.

As students begin to notice patterns in informants' speech styles —indicating that speakers of the English language are alike in their tendency to use standard forms more frequently in more formal settings—classroom discussions should offer students opportunities to discuss their individual and collective hypotheses explaining those patterns. Eventually, students will learn inductively what professional linguists have also learned inductively: Most speakers adjust their speech as they move from one situation to another. Additionally, and perhaps most significantly, students will become aware of the fact that most speakers employ nonstandard forms. Of course, early in their discussions, students will also note that many people have strong linguistic prejudices based on strong social prejudices.

The strategy described in this paper obviously will not cure all of the linguistic and social ills that victimize speakers of nonstandard dialects, but it accomplishes three goals. First, it helps students learn more about the English language and its users. That should remain a continual goal in all secondary and collegiate language arts classrooms. Second, it may encourage students who speak more highly regarded or standard dialects to become tolerant of nonstandard dialects and the speakers of those dialects. Third, it may help students who speak nonstandard dialects feel a little less linguistic insecurity and linguistic self-hatred, for while the strategy leads students to notice differences among speakers, it also helps them notice many similarities.

References

Burling, Robbins. *English in Black and White.* New York: Holt, Rinehart & Winston, 1973.

Joiner, Charles W. Martin Luther King Junior Elementary School Children, et al., Plaintiffs v. Ann Arbor School District Board, Defendant (Civil Action No. 7-71861). Ann Arbor, Michigan, 12 July 1979.

Labov, William. "Phonological Correlates of Social Stratification." *American Anthropologist* 66, no. 2 (1964): 164–176.

Sledd, James. "Bi-Dialectalism: The Linguistics of White Supremacy." *Challenge and Change in the Teaching of English.* Boston: Allyn and Bacon, 1971.

Using the Journal to Build Competence in Standard English

Dorothy Wells
Southern University in New Orleans

The value of journal writing in teaching composition has long been established.[1] This technique is especially effective for teachers who must deal either with basic writers or with writers who bring a nonstandard dialect into the classroom. Indeed, the students I have taught over the past twelve years fit into both categories: With few exceptions they speak some variant of a southern black dialect and they come out of public schools where they have been virtually untouched by instruction in the language arts. I originally introduced the journal into my classroom because I realized it would provide an excellent means for diagnosing students' particular difficulties and their individual dialectical forms. I soon learned that, in addition to serving this diagnostic purpose, the journal had several other effects so valuable as to take priority over my initial intentions.

After a decade of teaching in a predominantly black college, I had grown resigned to what I thought was an unavoidable barrier between myself, a white teacher, and my black students—unavoidable because of our language and cultural differences. The nature of this distance became particularly clear to me when I taught for a semester at a private university nearby, in a familiar setting with students I understood because I had been one of them not many years before. Here I rarely felt as though I misinterpreted classroom behavior. I knew what to make of the silent student sprawled out noncommittally in the back and I could easily handle the chatting girls in the front or the occasionally belligerent or critical student. In contrast, with students of a different culture I found it harder to interpret the behavioral cues. A white teacher is likely to interpret as hostile a sullen-looking face on a black student, particularly in the deep and urban South where hostility has become a way of life between the races. A group of chatty girls or a hostile student of a different culture were harder to deal

89

with than similar students of a familiar culture. That is, until I stumbled onto using the two-way journal in these classrooms.

As their journal assignment, I required students to write two pages in a spiral notebook for each class meeting and to submit their work weekly. I told them that I was not going to grade, or even pay attention to "grammar." I was reading only for content and I was going to write back to them in the journal. My initial reading of the journals convinced me that my investment of time was going to pay off. Indeed, I was rapidly able to determine the level of literacy of each student, far more rapidly than in conventional assignments. But a second result of the journals, and as it turned out, a more important one in its effect on my teaching, was that I quickly began to know each student in a far more intimate way than had ever been possible before. And they were able to know me in a dimension in which they were not used to knowing a teacher. I had promised them that the journal was to be absolutely private; they could write just about anything in it they wished and I would never allow anyone else to see its contents. It took only a couple of weeks for the students to begin to trust me in this assertion and to open up their lives in their journals.

Many times I was left wondering how to make a response that would not seem banal as I read their entries and had glimpses into lives fraught with the problems that poverty brings. But I always wrote back, careful to say something positive; perhaps I might comment on the clarity or vividness of their accounts, or on how interesting their experiences were. I might comment on the liveliness of the "voice" they brought to their journals or express my point of view in relation to one of their ideas. No longer were their faces and expressions a mystery to me, a cause for anxiety. With a much better sense of the reality behind the faces, I was able to relax as their teacher.

For example, last semester a group of aggressive girls sat together at the back of the classroom, chatted loudly and seeming on the surface to be hostile. (They quite possibly *were* hostile that first week of class.) But I soon came to know each of them through their journals; they were Venita (competent in many ways but impossibly inept in language skills), Danessa (a bit lazy but from a strict Catholic family where education was important), and Toni (eloquent about her neighborhood, which drug pushers ruled and where violence was common, and about her family, too large and not supportive of her desire to go to college). The chatting girls became in my mind a rather comic situation instead of a threatening one. The group was willing to accept my admonitions; I could joke that their behavior was kindergartenish without calling up hostility. Because they knew I respected their language and their lives, they were willing to respect mine. Thus, for me the most important use of the journal in teaching students who speak a nonstandard dialect is that it builds bridges between us. These bridges are no less important when a teacher has only a few students in the classroom who differ from the teacher culturally or linguistically.

The journal's second most important use is the help it offers students in discovering the vast amount of material they have available to them in their lives, a source for writing that few of them have ever been encouraged to tap. Although it takes a while to make basic writers or speakers of nonstandard dialects believe in the value of their own voices and experiences in an academic context, they soon begin to see that the writing in their journal is typically far better than what they attempt to do in their more formal assignments.

Slowly, I lead students to use their journals as a writer's notebook where they can explore and learn to trust in the materials and voices they have available to them. At first, the journal gets the students used to writing. The habits of literacy are virtually unpracticed in these students. They rarely read and even more rarely write. In their crowded and unruly high schools, little writing is required. As Mina Shaughnessy points out in *Errors and Expectations*, many need to practice even the basic motor movements associated with writing.[2] In addition, they need to learn the virtues of putting thoughts into words and onto paper. The journals do take time to read, but far less than a group of essays, and they are generally more interesting than the essays would be. Actually I look forward to sitting down to a set of journals because I anticipate in them a great variety of material and always the possibility of surprise. It is also a relief to attend to student writing as a reader and not as an evaluator. Here the teacher can relax in relationship to the material; there is no need to feel responsible for marking errors. And the students soon come to sense in the journals that the teacher is a pleasant participant, not a wielder of red pencils.

Typically, the first set of journals will be either the general autobiography an English teacher is so used to reading (of the "where I have lived," "where I went to school" variety) or an hour-by-hour skeletal account of a school day. After a couple of weeks, students begin to run out of general autobiographical material or tire of the repetitious day-by-day account. The teacher can then lead them into a discovery of the other material they can develop. I begin by suggesting areas each student might wish to explore. The students who typically describe only the bare events of the day can be encouraged to develop thoughts and ideas, to write of people, of specific details. I tell them about Joyce's *Ulysses*—how a whole novel can be written of a single day's experience. Slowly, most students begin to discover the material they have in their heads, material that can be used later in more formal types of classroom writing where examples or anecdotes are needed to flesh out an argument.

By far the best writing I get from my students, especially early in the semester, comes out of the journal. I have many examples that show a student writing incoherent, ungrammatical, flat, or unorganized prose in formal assignments while simultaneously managing pieces of elegant or vivid description in the journal. Of course, at some point they have to learn to write the kinds of prose acceptable in academic settings, but these students surely need to realize that the bits of exquisite description and narration they write in their journals are, when considered on a scale that takes into account the whole spectrum of written discourse, worth as much as academic prose. Once they see they are capable of good writing in one form they become less intimidated by other forms.

This semester I knew I had succeeded when I received my latest batch of out-of-class essays. In them I found the same pleasurable reading I had been encountering in the journals. My students had learned to transfer the conversational tone, the personal voices of the journals, into their more formal exercises in classification or comparison and contrast. The essays contained concrete details drawn from experience but used in the service of argument and exposition. In their teacher and in their classmates, they had found the sympathetic audience for whom they could be the genial and leisurely guide, with a few surprises up their sleeves.

And, finally, I have found that, as I originally intended, the journals offer an excellent opportunity to evaluate the real writing ability of each student. Here the writing students do is much closer to their actual voices than the writing they try to do in a more formal setting; thus, the teacher can develop a much clearer idea of what additional work each student needs to do to correct surface features of his or her writing. I give an individual spelling test to each student, drawn from the words misspelled in the journal. It makes more sense for them to learn the words they normally use rather than an arbitrary list suited to an imaginary student's needs.

After the journals are underway, I can begin using them to point out variations between dialect and standard English. In some journal entries I underline, in a distinctive color, places where the student is deviating from standard usage, omitting endings, or using vocabulary inappropriate to college writing. In conferences I ask students to read portions of their journals to me; I ask them to read in a "television announcer" voice, and usually, as they formalize their pronunciation, they hear the omitted *ed*'s and *s*'s and catch the auxiliary verb differences between their dialect and the standard version. As we know, developing the ability to code switch is a slow process, but the only way students will learn to do it is by coming to hear the standard code in their minds. All but the most dialect-bound students can learn to edit their own prose in this way.

Journals, creatively used, do enable students to improve their writing and, perhaps even more important, make them feel more positive about their abilities as writers. Because the journal is by nature a private medium, it can be used to help the isolated student in the classroom who speaks a nonstandard dialect without making him or her feel singled out from the other students. There is no question that using the journal is a time-consuming activity, but then, so is any other good method of teaching writing. I, for one, will never again teach composition without relying on the journal to acquaint me with my students and them with themselves.

Notes

1. See, for example, the section on the journal in Daniel Fader's *The New Hooked on Books* (New York: Berkley Books, 1976), pp. 70–79.

2. (New York: Oxford University Press, 1977), pp. 14–16.

Working with the
Hearing-impaired Child

Michael N. Milone, Jr.
James L. Collins
The Ohio State University

Because of recent legislation and improving attitutes toward handicapped persons, more and more hearing-impaired children are being placed in regular classroom settings. It is not often that these children are considered linguistically different, yet many of them are as unfamiliar with standard English as are immigrant or native-born speakers of foreign languages.

The hearing-impaired child is sometimes at an even greater disadvantage than other speakers of nonstandard English. A Vietnamese child, for example, may have well developed reading and writing skills in his or her native language. This strong foundation in Vietnamese can serve as a basis for the development of English. Many hearing-impaired children, in contrast, may have been reared in an environment in which neither English nor any form of sign language was encouraged. As a result, they do not have a strong foundation on which English competence can be built.

There are several general recommendations that regular classroom teachers can follow to foster the English language development of their hearing-impaired students. These recommendations are easily implemented, and often bring about marked improvement in written and spoken English. As a secondary benefit, they often contribute to improved social interaction between the hearing-impaired child and the other children in the class.

Remember that impaired hearing and underdeveloped English skills do not mean that a child is mentally retarded. Hearing-impaired children who are mainstreamed into regular education are almost always of average intelligence or better. Unfortunately, they are sometimes perceived as being mentally retarded because their speech is distorted and they misunderstand so many seemingly easy directions or conversations. The misperception of retardation causes adults and other children to talk down to hearing-impaired children, or even worse, to ignore them. The hearing-impaired child, in return, may withdraw from participation in the class or act out to gain the attention of the teacher.

One of the most effective ways of preventing this misunderstanding is for the teacher to spend some time with the class, explaining that the new student does not hear very well, and because of this condition, will not be able to speak clearly or understand everything that goes on in the classroom. Explain further that the hearing-impaired child is just as smart as everyone else in the class, but has not yet learned our language very well. A good example to use is the experience of an American child in a foreign classroom. He or she might be very smart, and yet be unable to understand what anyone is saying or explain anything to them.

A good demonstration of the effects of hearing impairment is to have half the children in a class watch a movie or television program without the sound, and have the other half watch it with sound. The group who watched with sound should then ask the other group some general and specific questions about the program. Another experience that sensitizes teachers and students to the situation of the hearing-impaired child is to wear attenuators of some kind, for example ear plugs, during a day in school.

Be sure the hearing-impaired child knows who is doing the talking in the room. One of the most frustrating situations hearing-impaired children and adults experience is tracking down the speaker in a rapid-fire exchange of words. No matter how hearing-impaired persons communicate, they can follow a lesson or conversation better if they know who the speaker is. They can then observe the speaker's face and mouth, and pick up many paraverbal cues that contribute to understanding the verbal message.

Have the members of the class hesitate before they speak in a group setting. This enables the hearing-impaired students to find and observe the speaker. At first it may help to have children point to the speaker; this practice will become unnecessary when the hearing-impaired child learns the flow of communication in the classroom.

There will always be some exchanges that are so rapid that the hearing-impaired child loses the thread of the conversation. If the topic is important, it is wise to stop the conversation and let the hearing-impaired child catch up. Many times, however, such transactions are not pertinent to the lesson and can be skipped over; even many of the normally hearing children in the class often miss these asides.

Take the time to explain popular slang terms, idioms, and figures of speech. Every language, including American sign language, is rich in slang terms, idioms, and figures of speech. These aspects of language add color, but are very difficult to master for non-native speakers of the language.

When these expressions appear in reading materials being used by the children, it is imperative that they be explained to the hearing-impaired student. Otherwise the student will never learn what they mean, will not understand the passage that was read, and may experience some confusion about the definition of the words that constitute the expression.

The problem is not so great when spoken expressions are used because they occur informally, and the hearing-impaired students usually have the opportunity to ask what they mean. Again, remind the students in the class that just because the hearing-impaired student asks about the meaning of common expressions does not indicate that the child is unintelligent. If the normally hearing children in the class take the time to explain the expressions they use, the hearing-impaired child soon picks up on them and uses them correctly.

Give the hearing-impaired child the chance to initiate interaction, but do not permit the child to monopolize the conversation. A new child in a strange classroom will be reluctant to initiate conversation or answer questions. Add to these factors the presence of a sensory disability, and it is easy to see why hearing-impaired children sometimes seem withdrawn, even in a classroom that has been well prepared for their coming. Patience, support, and encouragement are necessary to make the hearing-impaired child feel comfortable enough to risk initiating interaction. Once the child begins to initiate interaction, considerable social reinforcement should be provided to see that this tendency continues.

Some hearing-impaired children, however, have quite the opposite problem, and monopolize the conversation and the teacher's time in the classroom. These children have learned that when they have to react to what other people have said or done, they are at a disadvantage because of their hearing impairment. Rather than operate at a disadvantage, these children control the interactions in a classroom so that they can predict better what will come next.

The best way to deal with the hearing-impaired child who monopolizes the conversation is to respond in the same way you would to any other child who manifests similar behavior. Some teachers may have difficulty doing this because they are afraid of hurting the hearing-impaired child's feelings. Such reluctance is well intentioned, but only fosters a habit that will prevent the hearing-impaired child from developing receptive as well as expressive English language abilities.

When asking questions of hearing-impaired children, gradually increase their complexity. The questions that teachers ask contribute to students' thinking skills as well as their English language abilities. This is as true for hearing-impaired students as it is for their normally hearing peers. Auditorily disabled students, however, will have more difficulty understanding the question, and so may respond incorrectly even though they know the right answer. It is important, therefore, to teach hearing-impaired students to make sense of questions they are asked in the classroom.

To do this, begin by asking simple questions that require a yes or no answer. Follow by using questions that require brief, factual responses that are based on the child's experience or a recent lesson. Once the child can answer these fundamental questions correctly and confidently, you may ask open-ended questions that involve higher-order thinking skills. If you discover that the child has difficulty answering higher-order questions, drop down a level and ask a more simple question on a related topic. If the child answers this question correctly, he or she may be able to return to the more difficult one.

Normally hearing elementary school children acquire the ability to answer questions through years of informal interaction. It is unreasonable to expect hearing-impaired children, who are denied this opportunity, to acquire the ability to answer questions after only a few days of practice. It will take an extended period of persistent effort on the part of the teacher to bring hearing-impaired children up to the level of the rest of the class. The effort will be well worth it, however, for it will enable them to respond to questions in a manner that is commensurate with their true abilities.

Provide hearing-impaired children with ample feedback about their written and spoken language. Two factors that contribute significantly to English language development are modeling and feedback. Hearing-impaired children usually miss both of these, the first because of their sensory disability, and the second because so many normally hearing persons are reluctant to provide them with the feedback necessary to improve their language. There is little other than amplification that can be done about hearing impairment, but there is much that can be done to provide hearing-impaired children with feedback about their spoken and written English.

In providing feedback to hearing-impaired children, it is important to apply the same common-sense rules that you would use in promoting the language development of normally hearing children. Use generous doses of encouragement initially to foster self expression, both in speech or sign and in writing. Once the child has gained confidence, you can then begin to model correct language patterns and identify those that are incorrect. When you have reached this stage, be sure to continue the encouragement and reinforcement that will maintain high levels of self expression.

With normally hearing children, spoken language is almost always the springboard from which written expression is developed; this is also true for those hearing-impaired students who have well-developed language skills. For hearing-impaired children whose language is underdeveloped, however, the opposite may be true, and writing can be the vehicle through which spoken or signed language is developed. Writing is less capricious than speech; it provides ample opportunities for self-correction, and involves the visual and kinesthetic modalities. Working on a hearing-impaired child's written expression may prove more effective than working on the child's signed or spoken expression.

Whenever possible, use the same instructional materials for hearing-impaired students as you do with their classmates. One of the first tendencies many teachers have when they discover they will be working with a hearing-impaired child is to seek out specially designed materials. In some cases this is the correct thing to do, but in most instances this inclination defeats the whole purpose of mainstreaming. Hearing-impaired students who are chosen for mainstreaming invariably have the potential to use the same educational materials as the rest of the class. Denying the child the opportunity to use them adds to the restrictiveness of the environment and makes the child feel special in a negative way.

It is important to be sure that the hearing-impaired student understands how to complete the activities in a workbook. Another recommendation is to screen the vocabulary in a text before the child uses it, and be certain that the child knows the meaning of the terms that appear in the book.

A very effective instructional aid for hearing-impaired students is the computer. Language arts drill and practice materials provide them with the repetition they need to master English language skills, in a motivating way. Instructional programs cause less confusion than traditional print materials, and a computer provides the consistent feedback that is necessary for language learning.

Stress the basics. Hearing-impaired children need considerably more practice in the basics of English than their classmates. Handwriting, spelling, punctuation, grammar, and vocabulary cannot be overstressed with hearing-impaired children. These children must acquire in the classroom the fundamental language skills that their peers learned naturally as part of growing up. What's more, the hearing-disabled children must be exposed to the new English skills that the rest of the class is learning. In essence, hearing-impaired children must learn much more material than their peers, and must do so despite their sensory disability.

Do not be afraid to assign extra work to the hearing-impaired child, both in the classroom and at home. The work should be relevant, consist of many opportunities to practice, and should be sequential. The child should know how to complete the activities, and should be reinforced for hard work.

Use a checklist of some kind to chart the progress of the hearing-impaired student. This practice will ensure that essential skills are not overlooked, and will serve as a good framework within which instruction can be given.

Periodically review skills that the child has already learned, as the learning of some features of English can interfere with previously learned material. For example, when hearing-impaired children learn the passive voice, they may experience temporary confusion about the active voice. Reviewing the active voice will diminish this confusion.

Involve parents in the education of their hearing-impaired child. If you actively involve the parents of the hearing-impaired child in the educational process, you will have made an ally who will prove invaluable. These parents are often eager to help their child in any way they can, and are grateful for the opportunity to do so.

Parents can work with the child at home on assignments, seeing that the child understands the directions and is rewarded for his or her effort. They can keep you informed on how the child is using language in a natural setting, and will follow your advice on what experiences the child should have to facilitate English expression. They will support your efforts as far as they are able, and will sometimes be willing to buy any supplemental materials the child needs but are not available through the school because of budgetary constraints.

Take advantage of the resources that are available. There are several places to which teachers can turn for advice on how to improve the English skills of their hearing-impaired students:

Alexander Graham Bell Association for the Deaf; 3417 Volta Place, N.W.; Washington, DC 20007

Council for Exceptional Children; 1920 Association Drive; Reston, VA 22091

Gallaudet College; Washington, DC 20002

National Association of the Deaf; 814 Thayer Avenue; Silver Spring, MD 20910

From the points discussed on the preceding pages, it can be seen that fostering the English language development of hearing-impaired children in the regular classroom need not be a complicated proposition. True, there will always be times when an intervention to overcome the effects of the hearing impairment must be undertaken, but for the most part, sound educational practices developed for normally hearing children will work well with their hearing-impaired classmates. Remember that common sense is usually the best guide to working with hearing-impaired students, and that mastery of English results from an environment in which its use is encouraged.

Spelling and Grammar Logs

Richard VanDeWeghe
University of Colorado at Denver

One problem writing teachers face is that of helping students with their spelling and their use of edited English while developing their writing. A related problem is that of individualizing instruction in both areas in efficient and effective ways that keep both spelling and grammar in their "places" in the writing process. A solution to both problems is the use of spelling and grammar logs, two individualized, self-paced approaches which help students become more proficient at spelling and at using edited English. I have used the logs with university students, and I have helped other teachers use them with their junior high, high school, and college students. The logs work well with all students, but particularly well with linguistically or dialectically different students for whom spelling and grammar are special concerns in their writing development.

The spelling log is a one-page student handout divided into four labeled columns, with student examples (see figure 1). The spelling log is literally a log where students keep track of their misspellings during the copyediting stage of writing, or after others (teachers, parents, peers) have pointed out a misspelling.

I came upon the idea of spelling logs in Lou Kelly's fine text, *From Dialogue to Discourse*,[1] where her "Guide to Correct Spelling" uses the same format but does not include the second column. My addition of this column provides a visual contrastive analysis which allows students to *see* graphemic differences between the two versions. The third column is also instructive: Students write, in their own words, why they're confused. Coming as it does after the contrastive analysis, this is generally an easy task. Its strengths are that students explore the reason(s) for a misspelling in a personal, and hence more meaningful, chronicle, and that it combines thinking about and writing out the reason(s) in a risk-free, exploration and discovery way. Similarly, because the fourth-column entry represents a personal attempt at finding a cognitive key to the confusion, it locks in long-term memory of an individualized aid to remembering the correct spelling. Students thus do more than simply list misspelled words, for they must also analyze the correct spelling-misspelling confusion and find a mnemonic aid for fixing the correct spelling in their minds.

While it is best if students complete columns three and four themselves, they sometimes have difficulty determining a reason for the confusion or finding some aid for remembering the correct spelling. In such instances, teachers or others can help. For example, I've often had an entire class brainstorm a fourth-column entry for a student who just couldn't come up with something. These sessions are lively and instructive for all, since we've found that the best mnemonic aids are those that are silly or sing-songy. One student, in fact, remarked that he was amazed how well he could remember the "stupid sayings" in his spelling log.

Students work well with the spelling log because it formalizes a spelling strategy that many people do informally or unconsciously. And because it calls on students to write their way to personal solutions, they retain the resultant learning more readily. Further, teachers can quickly and easily monitor students' use of the log by examining it periodically. This provides teachers an opportunity to spot patterns in spelling problems and then to develop specific strategies for dealing with them (for example, applying the *ei-ie* rule). The log works best for fair to somewhat poor spellers who spell correctly the greater percentage of words they write. For severely handicapped spellers (I once had a student who misspelled 85 percent of the words he wrote), I recommend

Correct Spelling	My Misspelling	Why the Word Confuses Me	Helps for Remembering the Correct Spelling
meant	ment	I spell it like I think it sounds.	It's the past of *mean*.
demonstrate	demenstrate	I use *e* instead of *o*.	A dem*o* is used to dem*o*nstrate.
coarse	course	I get it mixed up with course as a class.	*a* = co*a*rse is h*a*rd.

Figure 1. Spelling log.

Mina Shaughnessy's more systematic spelling analysis in her book, *Errors and Expectations.*[2]

Here are some student entries which illustrate their use of the spelling log. Student A recorded *angle* as a misspelling of *angel*, noted that "I get the *l* and the *e* mixed up," and then wrote his marvelous memory help: "Angels have *gel* in them." Student B noted "famialy or famaly" as the misspelling of *family;* he said he was confused "because of the way [he says] it," and then devised his personal memory link in "*i* am in a fam*i*ly." Student C spelled *committee* as either "comitte" or "commity," noting that she "only hears one *t* or forgets the other *e*." Her mnemonic aid was simple and rhythmical: "2 *m*'s, 2 *t*'s, 2 *e*'s." Finally, student D wrote *holler* as "hollar," explaining that "That's how [she says] it," and then wrote that she could remember it by saying, "When you holl*er*, you *ger*."

While resembling the spelling log in form, function, and use, the grammar log[3] is a descriptive rather than prescriptive approach to helping students analyze how their personal grammar (spoken language and informal written language) differs from their written grammar (edited English conventions). I am using *grammar* here in its broadest lay sense to include syntax, punctuation, usage, and vocabulary. Divided into three columns, the grammar log is exemplified in figure 2.

Students use the grammar log as they use the spelling log—to chart and analyze discrepancies between personal and written grammars. Unlike the spelling log entries, however, there are no "incorrect" entries (with the exception of punctuation) in the grammar log; the only judgments to be made are those of appropriateness. Thus, when students enter syntactic structures in their logs (for example, "I wonder how can I accomplish this?" versus "I wonder how I can accomplish this?"), they are actually recording

Personal Grammar	Written Grammar	Reasons for Differences
my brothers house	my brother's house	I need to put in an apostrophe (') to show ownership.
We took the following items, a camera, a backpack, and a canteen.	We took the following items: a camera, a backpack, and a canteen.	I should use a colon (:) when I introduce a series of things.

Figure 2. Grammar log.

linguistic styles more or less appropriate to social situations. Because the grammar log is descriptive, no value judgments are thus placed on students' personal grammars. In fact, when teachers explain to students the meanings of personal and written grammars, they need to emphasize that people have a variety of personal grammars, and illustrate this fact by drawing examples from their own idiolects or dialects. Further, teachers need to emphasize that personal grammar is natural to the idea-generating nature of the drafting phases of writing, and that the application of written grammar structures and conventions comes in the editing phase. This introduction thus maintains the students' right to their own language, and, if handled properly, shows them the "place" of their personal grammar in the total writing process when an edited English style is the desired goal.

While the contrastive analysis in columns one and two allows students to see the differences, arriving at reasons for the differences helps them to learn the "rules" we often teach, but in an individualized, situation-specific way. Their rules, assuming they're accurate, can be in their own words or they may be paraphrases of comments made by teachers or others. Merely copying a rule from a handbook is wasted rote transcription and is to be avoided. The important point is that the process of arriving at reasons for the differences, and the process of writing them out combine to promote genuine understanding of punctuation, grammar, and usage principles. And in the process, students often pick up common terms that identify features of edited English (for example, punctuation signals, grammatical markers).

Some examples: Student A's writing contained many features of black dialect. In his log, he noted in the personal grammar column the phrase "that he be a fine . . ."; in the written grammar column, he logged in "that will be a fine . . .". Similarly, he noted that "I wonder did . . ." in his personal grammar was "I wonder if . . ." in his written grammar. His reason for both entries was simply the differences in the way he spoke and the way he should have written in the final draft of a college paper. Student B wrote that "they gained and unyielding critic" in her personal grammar became "they gained an unyielding critic" in her written grammar because she could *see* the differences that she couldn't *hear*. Student C, who noted that in her personal grammar she referred to an "older-held view," logged in "traditional view" at a peer's suggestion because "it was a better way to say it." Finally, Student D wrote that "there was fifteen students in class" was all right for his personal grammar, but "there were fifteen students" is more appropriate in his written grammar because "*was* is used with one thing and *were* is used with a few."

Spelling and grammar logs supplement a writing course. They should be seen as an opportunity for students to find solutions to problems they face in these two areas without distracting them from their natural writing processes. The logs also provide an opportunity for teachers to monitor students' development, discover patterns in spelling and grammar, and attend to incidental problems that do not form patterns. Used as an aid in copyediting, logs can, and do, develop genuine student understanding of correct spelling and appropriate grammar.

Notes

1. Lou Kelly, *From Dialogue to Discourse* (Glenview, Ill.: Scott Foresman, 1972), p. 323.

2. Mina Shaughnessy, *Errors and Expectations* (New York: Oxford University Press, 1977), pp. 175–176.

3. I first began working with the idea of grammar logs in an inservice project in language arts at Michigan State University, Department of English—Sturgis, Michigan, Middle School. The final report of that project is *Beyond Basics* (East Lansing: Michigan State University, 1977).

Dialect Differences
in the Composition Class

Karen L. Greenberg
Hunter College, CUNY

The students in my college freshman composition classes have common goals: to extend and refine their writing skills and to acquire greater control over the options and resources of standard written English. While these two goals are different, the strategies and processes used to achieve them are quite similar and capitalize on students' differences.

Although they are in the same kind of composition class, my students are at very different points on a wide continuum representing skill in writing. They differ greatly in their writing experiences, degree of interest and motivation, cognitive style, and rate of learning. In addition, each student has different linguistic resources: Each speaks and writes his or her idiosyncratic mixture of regional, social, or racial varieties of English. To make optimal use of this heterogeneity, I have to create opportunities for the students to talk and write together in small groups so that they can benefit from one another's competencies.

Arranging and facilitating these small-group experiences has become much easier over the past five years, thanks largely to the excellent techniques and tasks presented in such books as Thom Hawkins's *Group Inquiry Techniques for Teaching Writing* (National Council of Teachers of English, 1976) and Ken Bruffee's *A Short Course in Writing* (Winthrop, 1972).

Grouping students with different linguistic and social backgrounds fosters language experimentation in a "natural" setting. To communicate with their peers, students must use (or learn) mutually acceptable forms in speaking and in writing. Furthermore, group reactions to a student's writing create a consensus and make criticisms easier to heed because these no longer represent one person's (usually the teacher's) value judgments.

Students who work together in a small group help each other to extend the range of their language and form discourse in more meaningful ways. They provide one another with immediate feedback about the ways in which their errors impede the reader's understanding of their written meanings.

In addition to writing for one another and evaluating each other's compositions, students in my classes do other small-group activities. One of these is a field study of usage patterns in writing, and this particular activity is designed to increase students' awareness of linguistic options. Each group decides on the particular "source" that it wants to study and then collects writing samples from that source. During the past few semesters, these sources have included textbooks, handbooks, newspapers, magazines, journals, comic books, student essays, student letters, teacher assignments, and transcriptions of speeches and conversations.

After all of the data are collected, the groups analyze the characteristics of the writing samples and present reports on these characteristics to the entire class. For example, this semester we discussed the ways in which the sources differed in terms of their paragraph organizations, sentence structures, and verb tenses.

This kind of linguistic exploration and analysis always leads to discussions of language attitudes and of the sociopolitical and socioeconomic aspects of language use. As students compare the structures in the different sources, they develop a clearer understanding of language standards and an awareness of the many ways in which dialects change to fit the writer's purpose and the perceived reader.

Several of my classes have become so interested in the linguistic explorations discussed above that they broadened their studies to include oral and written surveys of the language attitudes of other students, family members, and community members. These have resulted in individual and group reports on the sociocultural dimensions of language behvaior.

This kind of group discussion plus composition activity creates its own motivation for writing and editing because it arises from students' curiosity about language. As students analyze and synthesize the results of their surveys, they must listen to and read each other's ideas and dialects and provide each other with immediate and abundant feedback. And most important, they are increasing their awareness and appreciation of their language differences and their linguistic choices.

Sarah Jones: A Teaching Case Study

Steven M. Culver
Virginia Polytechnic Institute and State University

Sarah Jones (a fictitious name) is an eighteen-year-old black girl who was enrolled in one of my basic writing courses on the university level. Sarah was just one of many students I had in my first years as a teacher of writing, and I am sure that I learned at least as much from them as they learned from me. I present this case study for the benefit of those other teachers who, in attacking the problems of inexperienced writers, try numerous and varied approaches to them.

The first problem was to deal with Sarah's attitude about writing in general, and her writing in particular. She did not have a "bad" attitude; she wasn't sullen, moody, or unhappy. On the contrary, she was usually bright and extremely cheerful. Her happy mood, though, was more than simply contentment or bliss through ignorance. She was painfully aware of her limitations, and her smiling demeanor was simply a defense mechanism; she was ready to see errors pointed out to her even before she had finished writing. When, as expected, these errors were made evident to her, she laughed them off as "stupid" or "silly" mistakes.

Sarah's attitude created two problems that had to be taken care of: (1) She demonstrated a complete lack of confidence in her writing abilities; and (2) she had to be made to see that these mistakes of hers were not silly or stupid, but were just the opposite—important deviations from standard written English that had to be corrected. The paradox was obvious: I had to instill within Sarah the confidence she desperately needed to improve her writing, and yet at the same time I had to show her that the mistakes in her writing were grave, not silly, ones, that greatly affected her ability to communicate on paper.

The first step in solving this sphinxian question was to have as much contact time with Sarah as possible, to allow her to become

comfortable with me, and to give me a chance to know her problems and attitudes better. This constant attitude monitoring was
important because of Sarah's frustration with the composition
process. She had already had numerous failures, and she now
believed that writing was a magical ability granted an individual
through heredity or environment (an attitude that is typical of
basic writers, according to Shaughnessy). To combat this attitude
I showed Sarah copies of Ernest Hemingway's manuscript of *A
Farewell to Arms*. Hemingway rewrote the ending of the novel
almost thirty times before he wrote the published version. This
ending and the rest of the manuscript are filled with crossed-out
words, words written above words, and sentences rewritten,
scratched out, and rearranged. By looking at this, Sarah (I hoped)
would get the idea that writing was more hard work than magical
talent. She was, I believe, at least partially convinced, though in
retrospect, I think it would have been more practical and more
convincing if I had shown her a fellow student's writing and
editing, rather than a published author's. I think she would have
felt a stronger sense of identification with the former.

Working with her own papers, I showed Sarah where she could
make changes to improve her writing. Carefully avoiding words
like "mistake" and "error," I pointed out to her how certain mechanical conventions in her writing might cause confusion on the
part of the reader. To emphasize my point, I had Tony, another
freshman and another black student in my basic writing class,
come to my office when Sarah would be there. I chose another
black student for two reasons: Tony had the same kinds of mechanical problems as Sarah did, and I wanted to avoid any hint of a
racial difference related to my "editing" of Sarah's papers. The
reason for avoiding, and therefore not acknowledging, the question of skin color was purely practical. I did not want Sarah to fall
back on the "black dialect" excuse, as Tony was in the habit of
doing; it provides an easy out for a black student who says, "I
know my verb tenses, but my black dialect intrudes into my thinking once in a while; there's really nothing I can do about that."
With Tony and Sarah reading each other's papers during a conference, the dialect problem was put in its proper light: a barrier
to communication.

Perhaps I should explain here the particulars of their dialect
problems. Even though both Tony and Sarah often wrote using
verb forms acceptable in so-called black English and unacceptable
in standard written English, they did recognize the differences

between the two standards; they simply did not recognize them in their own papers. When reading each other's papers, however, both Sarah and Tony could pick out any informal verb forms and transpose them into standard English. Gradually they were weaned back onto their own papers, where they found errors more consistently than before, though still not with complete accuracy.

I assigned journals every week, four entries of at least 150 words each, to give students a chance to practice their writing. Sample topics for the journal included such subjects as "Virginia Tech on a winter's morning," "Why I hate or love my roommate," "If I could be an animal, which one would I be?" and "My favorite meal." Not only did students get to practice writing in their journals, but they also had to practice new concepts that they had learned in class. Sometimes, for example, I stipulated that a particular journal entry be written in past tense. This practice idea boomeranged with the introduction of semicolons. In one journal entry, I requested that the students use at least two semicolons correctly. As Shaughnessy says, this assignment did nothing but cause semicolons to appear virtually everywhere. Sarah was no exception, and it took me a couple of weeks to get her to again use periods to end her sentences.

With all of this writing, if Sarah had any problems they were bound to crop up, and crop up they did. The first writing Sarah did for me was an in-class essay the first day of class. Titled "The First Impressions" the essay was written in response to the question, "How has a quarter of school changed your views of Virginia Tech?" It certainly set the tone for the rest of the quarter. The first paragraph follows:

> When I walk upon the campus grounds of Virginia Tech. I knew right then, that I would receive my college degree here. The campus seem large and breathtaking to me. I would never meet the same people everyday. By me knowing that it gets extremely cold here in the winter. I wanted to become a part of this coldness. Fall quarter has greatly changed my first impressions toward Virginia Tech.

Though Sarah began her essay with a fragment and stumbled awkwardly through the introduction, she did finish with an answer to the framed question—yes, fall quarter had changed her impressions of Virginia Tech. A wisp of organization and thought was noticeable in the paragraph. Another important point in Sarah's favor was that, because she had already had one quarter of basic writing, she knew the vocabulary involved with grammatical concepts. Most of the time she knew the basics: what is meant by "agreement," what are subjects and predicates, and whether a subject is singular or plural. When I discussed this first paper with her, I did not need to start from square one. A third point in Sarah's favor was that she wrote on a more sophisticated structural level than many basic writing students, or perhaps, on a stronger rhetorical base than most other basic students. Rather than repeating the same structures over and over, Sarah varied her sentences. The first sentence, for example, begins with an adverbial clause. True, it is punctuated as a sentence, but it demonstrates a freedom from the basic writer's repetitive prose: "I did this . . . I did that . . . I went here . . . I saw her . . . and I went home."

During the quarter I knew of no other way to help Sarah correct her problem with punctuating dependent clauses as sentences but to drill her over and over on recognizing conjunctions. I don't know whether it was my insistence or her determination to get me off her back, but she made no such mistakes on her final exam for the quarter; every introductory adverbial clause had a comma after it, connecting it to the independent clause that followed. Other than punctuation, she had no problems with these clauses; they were rarely misplaced.

Another problem of Sarah's that is symptomatic of many basic writers is that she loved the world of generalities. For example, if one had to find Virginia Tech from her details given in her paragraph on "The First Impressions," it would be almost impossible; Tech would be a "large" place that is "cold." Her in-class exercises were almost always written on the general level with few specifics included.

In *Zen and the Art of Motorcycle Maintenance,* Pirsig presents a solution for the writer who cannot be specific enough and so has little to write. He proposes that students look not at the town, not at the main street of the town, not at a building on the main street of town, and not at a wall of a building on the main street of town. Rather, the writer must look first at the brick in one particular place on the wall of a building on the main street of the town. From this section of brick, the student writer can easily go on to the wall, the building, the main street, and finally to other parts of the town. I tried this approach with Sarah and it seemed to help. One assignment I gave her required her to talk about her favorite sandwich:

My favorite sandwich is the Spam-Ham-Treat Delight. It is held together by three slices of soft, whole white bread. On the outside slices one side is covered with my favorite types of spreads. The order of these spreads is: mayonnaise, mustard, ketchup, and relish.

These first three sentences of her essay indicate that she achieved a measure of specificity by listening to my advice. Just for fun, I had her write as many words as she could on each part of the sandwich. When she found that she could take half a page of paper and fill it with details about the bread on her sandwich, writing became an enjoyable exercise for her. Consequently (I like to think), her writing seemed to improve.

Sarah's problems were similar to those of many basic writers. She lacked confidence in her ability to communicate on paper; she often wrote in generalities rather than in specifics; and she was more familiar with a nonstandard dialect than with the accepted standard. Through students like Sarah, I have gradually come to learn what teaching strategies can work most effectively with students who have trouble with the standard dialect. I have also learned the most important lesson—that it takes a number of different strategies to teach writing effectively to even one student.